TRADE ISSUES, POLICIES AND LAWS

US-CHINA TRADE

PERSPECTIVES AND IMPACT ON THE GLOBAL ECONOMY

TRADE ISSUES, POLICIES AND LAWS

Additional books and e-books in this series can be found on Nova's website under the Series tab.

TRADE ISSUES, POLICIES AND LAWS

US-CHINA TRADE

PERSPECTIVES AND IMPACT ON THE GLOBAL ECONOMY

JOHN C. AMON
EDITOR

nova
science publishers
New York

Library of Congress Cataloging-in-Publication Data

ISBN: 978-1-53619-956-7

Published by Nova Science Publishers, Inc. † New York

CONTENTS

PREFACE

The United States of America and the Peoples' Republic of China are the world's leading economies. As such, if one wishes to understand the global economy, he or she must consider the economic relationship between these two countries. Chapter one examines the complex trade interrelationship among the US, China, and Africa, and the impact this system has on Africa's development. Chapter two analyzes the overall situation of the development of the Sino-US trade by examining the history of trade between China and the US starting from the late 18th century. Chapter three provides an overview of the trade war between China and the United States and illustrates the impact of this conflict on Latin America.

Chapter 1 - Both the USA and China have preferential trade facilitating arrangements that promote certain products from Africa to enter their respective markets duty free. Several indexes were used to examine how these two countries trade with Africa and the implications thereof for Africa's industrial development through trade. The intra-industry trade index shows the extent to which there is two-way trade in high value-added manufactured goods between trading partners as this type of trade has implications for technology transfer and modernising industrial bases. Results show that, it is in the USA-Africa trade where there are more and sustainable intra-industry trade opportunities and potential, and thus more relevant in helping African countries to develop their industries further through technology transfers, an interchange of knowledge and joint research. The revealed trade preference index examines the extent to which trading partners regard each other as significant trading partners. The results show that China and Africa regard each other as significant trading partners as their trade is significantly oriented towards each other, and the extent of this orientation has been rising over the years. Trade intensity and orientation between the USA and Africa has been on a constant decline, with such a decline accelerating even faster after 2012. Therefore, it is China which has been harnessing and utilising more fully trade opportunities that arise in Africa. The revealed trade barriers index gives insights into the ease with which products from various regions can access a market. The results show that most raw materials, resource-intensive goods and low-value added goods imported by the USA and China experience preferential treatment when entering both markets. High value-added manufactured goods are mainly discriminated against upon entry into either the USA or China. However, the level of discrimination is experienced a lot more when entering the Chinese market than the USA market. Therefore, it is the USA, which provides Africa with more room and easier market access for high MVA products, thus giving Africa an incentive to continue to modernise and improve the technological complexity of its manufactured products. This is important for Africa so that it does not continue to remain largely as an import source for raw materials and low value-added manufactured goods. The trade complementarity index shows the extent to which trading partners' export supplies match each other's import demand as well as to highlight product areas in which trade can be developed further by trading partners. The results show that both the USA and China's export supplies match Africa's import demand very well. This shows that, across all product categories, there are potentials for Africa to develop further its trade relations with both countries. However, the results on this show that it is with China that Africa has been developing further its trade in some of the product categories, and not the USA. The product categories in which Africa has been doing this with China are Chemicals, Machinery and transport equipment where it can obtain medium-skill and high-skill technology-intensive inputs and final goods.

Chapter 2 - This research analyzes the overall situation of the development of the Sino-US trade. First, the evolution process of Sino-US trade relations is sorted out and divided into four stages: Sino-US trade review from the Qing Dynasty to the Second World War; Sino-US trade review from the Second World War to the establishment of the People's Republic of China; Sino-US trade review from the establishment of the People's Republic of China to the establishment of Sino-US diplomatic relations; the development and change of Sino-US trade after the establishment of Sino-US diplomatic relations. Second, from the perspective of total trade volume, China's trade surplus with the U.S has been constantly increasing, which indicates that Chinese exports are increasingly dependent on the American market, and aggravates the asymmetry of Sino-US trade relations. The asymmetry of Sino-US trade relations has also brought great uncertainty and risk to the development of China's economy and foreign trade. Finally, the trade imbalance between China and the U.S. is the major obstacle to the development of Sino-U.S. trade relations as well as the direct cause of Sino-US trade war.

Chapter 3 – The authors present an overview of the trade war between China and the United States, highlighting the factors that have led to the current conflict. Subsequently, the authors discuss the key potential impacts on the two competitors, briefly analyzing the probable consequences not only on China and the United States but also on the world, particularly the Latin American countries. The authors illustrate how the trade flows of selected Latin American and Caribbean countries (LACs) complement each other and examine the possible scenarios for the relationship between China, the US, and the LACs in light of the new US Administration.

In: US-China Trade
Editor: John C. Amon
ISBN: 978-1-53619-956-7

Chapter 1

UNITED STATES OF AMERICA-AFRICA TRADE AND CHINA-AFRICA TRADE: A COMPARISON AND IMPLICATIONS FOR AFRICA'S INDUSTRIAL DEVELOPMENT THROUGH TRADE

Tsitsi Effie Mutambara [*] ***and Malwande Ndzabukelwako*** [†]
Rhodes University, Makhanda, Republic of South Africa

ABSTRACT

Both the USA and China have preferential trade facilitating arrangements that promote certain products from Africa to enter their respective markets duty free. Several indexes were used to examine how these two countries trade with Africa and the implications thereof for Africa's industrial development through trade. The intra-industry trade index shows the extent to which there is two-way trade in high value-added manufactured goods between trading partners as this type of trade has

---

[*] Corresponding Author's E-mail: t.e.mutambara@ru.ac.za.
[†] Corresponding Author's E-mail: Malwande.ndzabukelwalo@gmail.com.

implications for technology transfer and modernising industrial bases. Results show that, it is in the USA-Africa trade where there are more and sustainable intra-industry trade opportunities and potential, and thus more relevant in helping African countries to develop their industries further through technology transfers, an interchange of knowledge and joint research. The revealed trade preference index examines the extent to which trading partners regard each other as significant trading partners. The results show that China and Africa regard each other as significant trading partners as their trade is significantly oriented towards each other, and the extent of this orientation has been rising over the years. Trade intensity and orientation between the USA and Africa has been on a constant decline, with such a decline accelerating even faster after 2012. Therefore, it is China which has been harnessing and utilising more fully trade opportunities that arise in Africa. The revealed trade barriers index gives insights into the ease with which products from various regions can access a market. The results show that most raw materials, resource-intensive goods and low-value added goods imported by the USA and China experience preferential treatment when entering both markets. High value-added manufactured goods are mainly discriminated against upon entry into either the USA or China. However, the level of discrimination is experienced a lot more when entering the Chinese market than the USA market. Therefore, it is the USA, which provides Africa with more room and easier market access for high MVA products, thus giving Africa an incentive to continue to modernise and improve the technological complexity of its manufactured products. This is important for Africa so that it does not continue to remain largely as an import source for raw materials and low value-added manufactured goods. The trade complementarity index shows the extent to which trading partners' export supplies match each other's import demand as well as to highlight product areas in which trade can be developed further by trading partners. The results show that both the USA and China's export supplies match Africa's import demand very well. This shows that, across all product categories, there are potentials for Africa to develop further its trade relations with both countries. However, the results on this show that it is with China that Africa has been developing further its trade in some of the product categories, and not the USA. The product categories in which Africa has been doing this with China are Chemicals, Machinery and transport equipment where it can obtain medium-skill and high-skill technology-intensive inputs and final goods.

1. INTRODUCTION

The United States of America and the Peoples' Republic of China are the world's leading economies. Both countries have strong diplomatic ties to Africa, and they continue to reinforce this relationship. Initial relations with the Continent were driven by both countries' geopolitical and diplomatic interests. Both countries were not part of the initial "Scramble for Africa" during the colonial era that was spearheaded by the European powers, however, they are the most influential players in the neo-colonial Scramble for Africa. Nowadays the USA-Africa and China-Africa relationships are primarily driven by their economic needs (especially the need to secure stable oil and energy supplies, as well as resources, especially mineral resources) than political needs; although Mulualem (2014) claims that, the USA has more security and political interests in African than economic interests. This can be supported by the USA military presence in Africa to protect its national interests, and Cooke (2013:viii) notes that this is through the establishment of the USA combat command for Africa, i.e., the US Africa Command (AFRICOM) which seeks to reorder and re-priorotise US military engagement in Africa.

This chapter compares and contrasts China and the USA's engagements with Africa with regard to trade. With China's rise in global trade, it has intensified its trade links with Africa, just as it has done with other parts of the world. In this regard therefore, it would be interesting to examine and see how the USA has responded with regard to its trade engagements with the African Continent. Therefore, in this research paper, China-Africa trade and USA-Africa trade were examined and compared with regard to (i) the types of products the two countries import from- and export to Africa, and the implications this has on industrial development of the continent. The underlining theoretical debates that help to explain such trade patterns were examined and the implications for industrial development; (ii) prospects and opportunities for intra-industry trade in China and the USA trade with Africa were also examined, as this form of trade has important and significant implications for helping African countries to develop further their industrial bases as well as to create and pursue dynamic comparative advantages; (iii) the extent to which both China and USA trade is oriented towards the African continent and whether there have been any changes in such an orientation; (iv) the extent to which, from Africa's perspective, China and the USA export supplies complement Africa's import demand, and whether on seeing sectors in which trade with China and the USA could be developed further, Africa has taken the initiatives to further develop such trade with these two countries. High trade complementarity show that it is possible for bilateral trade to be developed even further between countries. Harnessing opportunities identified where trade can be developed further has significant implications for industrial development, especially where this encourages the inflow of medium-skill and high-skill and technology-intensive goods (both inputs and final goods) as this helps in technology transfer that is needed to modernise and develop a country's industrial base.

This chapter is organised as follows: Section 2 examines and discusses some of the major trade instruments used by China and the USA to engage Africa with regard to improving and promoting trade with the African Continent. Section 3 presents and discusses the methodology, techniques and procedures used in generating empirical evidence to compare and contrast China-Africa trade and USA-Africa trade. Section 4 presents the results and brings out the implications of such results for Africa's industrial development through trading with China and the USA. Section 5 concludes the chapter.

2. How the USA and China Engage Africa with Regard to Trade

Both the USA and China have preferential trade agreements with African countries, particularly Sub-Saharan African (SSA) countries. These trade agreements allow certain products from qualifying trade partners to enter the USA and the Chinese market duty free through specific favourable bilateral trade agreements and other trade facilitating measures.

Additionally, both countries provide substantial aid, investments and loans to the Continent as well as various forums for cooperation and discussions.

2.1. Instruments through Which the USA Facilitates Trade with Africa

The USA promotes trade with Africa through the Africa Growth and Opportunity Act (AGOA) program; the Generalised System of Preferences (GSP) program; Trade and Investment Framework Agreements (TIFAs) with Western African countries, Eastern and Southern African countries, as well as other countries; as well as initiating Free Trade Agreement negotiations with, e.g., the Southern African Customs Union. The preferential access these trade-facilitating measures promote are beneficial to African countries as they create an enabling trading environment and create new markets for eligible African products. Furthermore, duty free entry of products, especially those that serve as inputs to American companies, boosts American products' competitiveness by reducing the costs of imported inputs used to manufacture goods in the United States. This is particularly so for several small businesses in the United States, many of which rely on these programs' duty savings to stay competitive.

2.1.1. The African Growth and Opportunity Act (AGOA)

The most notable United States instrument aimed to facilitate trade engagements with Africa is the African Growth and Opportunity Act (AGOA) signed in May 2000 to promote trade relations with Africa. In 2015, the USA Congress passed legislation modernising and extending the AGOA program to 2025. AGOA provides preferential access to the USA market for selected products from qualifying Sub-Saharan African countries, thus providing new market opportunities for African exports. By providing duty-free entry into the United States for almost all African products, the Office of the United States Trade Representative (2020) notes that this initiative thus helped to expand and diversify exports originating from Africa that could enter the USA market duty free, as a lot more products were already eligible for duty free under the USA Generalised System of Preferences program. Examples of specific benefits, which have accrued to African countries from the AGOA program, include significant increases in exports of apparel to the United States from countries such as Kenya, Lesotho, Madagascar, Mauritius, Eswatini, and Ethiopia. African countries have also taken advantage of the AGOA program to include exporting other products, including value-added agricultural products and specialty food items such as macadamia nuts and chili sauces; cut flowers (largely from East Africa); and manufactured goods such as sunglasses and footwear. Notably, South Africa has utilised the program to export the widest array of products under AGOA, ranging from passenger vehicles to citrus products to frozen sorbet. As noted by UNCTAD (2018), Office of the United States Trade Representative (2020) and Jones and Williams (2012:15), very few African countries are not beneficiaries, and as of 2020, Office of the United States Trade Representative (2020:79) notes that 38 African countries were eligible for the AGOA programme[1].

2.1.2. The Generalised Systems of Preferences (GSP)

The GSP is the largest and oldest USA preferential trade treatment program where certain products are eligible for duty-free entry to the USA under specific qualifications. This trade preference program seeks to promote economic development by eliminating duties on thousands of products when imported from designated beneficiary countries in Least Developed Countries (LDCs). By creating an enabling trading environment for developing countries, this program, thus helps beneficiary countries to increase and diversify their trade with the United States. By granting duty-free and quota-free market access for exports of LDCs, this in turn promotes productive capacity development in the beneficiary countries and increased trade. UNCTAD (2018:2-9) and Office of the United States Trade Representative (2019a:14) note that, to date, very few African countries are

[1] Burundi, Cameroon, DRC, Eritrea, Mauritania, South Sudan and Zimbabwe are not eligible. Equatorial Guinea and Seychelles graduated from the program and are no longer eligible, while Somalia and Sudan were not reviewed for eligibility, as they neither requested for designation as an AGOA beneficiary country (Office of the United States Trade Representative, 2020:79).

not beneficiaries, and these are Equatorial Guinea, Libya, Morocco, Seychelles and Sudan.

2.1.3. Trade and Investment Framework Agreements (TIFAs)

Trade and Investment Framework Agreements (TIFAs) provide strategic frameworks and principles for dialogue on trade and investment issues between the United States and countries at different levels of development. TIFA Councils normally meet at least once a year at senior levels of government, thus providing a forum to meet and discuss issues of mutual interest with the objective of improving cooperation and enhancing opportunities for trade and investment. Market access issues are of particular importance when it comes to dialogue on trade (Office of the United States Trade Representative, 2019b).

To facilitate trade with Africa through TIFAs, the USA does so with individual countries, as well as with the regional economic integration arrangements in Africa. To this effect, the Office of the United States Trade Representative (2019b) notes that the United States of America has concluded several TIFAs with African countries and regional groups. With specific countries, TIFAs have been concluded with Algeria, Angola, Egypt, Ghana, Liberia, Libya, Mauritius, Mozambique, Rwanda, Nigeria, South Africa and Tunisia. The USA has also concluded TIFAs with regional economic integration arrangements in Africa, e.g., the Common Market for Eastern and Southern Africa (COMESA), the East African Community (EAC), Economic Community of West African States (ECOWAS) and the West African Economic Monetary Union (WAEMU).

2.2. Instruments through Which China Facilitates Trade with Africa

China-Africa economic and trade cooperation is a major component of South-South cooperation, and contributes towards infusing new life into trade between regions in the southern Hemisphere. China's trade engagements with Africa is promoted by the trade facilitating platforms and instruments which China has put in place to promote China-Africa trade. Such initiatives are the Forum on China-Africa Cooperation (FOCAC), bilateral trade agreements entered into with various African countries, China's Duty-Free Quota-Free (DFQF) Programme, as well as other trade facilitating measures. Therefore, as People's Republic of China State Council (2010) argues, China and Africa take initiatives to utilise more fully the complementary advantages in each other's resources and economic structures.

2.2.1. Forum on China–Africa Cooperation (FOCAC)

The Forum on China–Africa Cooperation (FOCAC) was established in 2000. People's Republic of China State Council (2010) says that, joint efforts by both China and Africa have made FOCAC an important platform for collective dialogue and an effective mechanism for practical cooperation between China and Africa. FOCAC enhances political mutual trust; promotes cooperation, especially economic and trade cooperation; and expands and deepens China-Africa relations through fostering diplomatic and institutional relationships with African nations.

Mutambara (2016:52) notes that FOCAC is most notable for facilitating China's trade engagements with Africa because driven by the FOCAC, subsequent FOCAC meetings/conferences have been held to strengthen and deepen economic and trade cooperation. Thus, other initiatives have been set up to foster China-Africa economic and trade linkages, e.g., (i) the China-Africa Joint Chamber of Commerce set up in 2006; (ii) the Conference of Chinese and African Entrepreneurs; and (iii) the China-Africa Joint Business Council founded in 2000. The Beijing Summit also provided a platform for China to form new strategic partnerships with Africa regarding new trade and infrastructure agreements. Therefore, especially since the establishment of FOCAC in 2000, economic and trade cooperation has been enhanced further and revitalised.

Among other things, cooperation on trade issues feature prominently in the various Memorandums of Understanding (MOUs) signed between China and African countries under the auspice of the Belt and Road Initiative and FOCAC. Viljoen (2019) notes that some of the projects in the MOUs which have a direct effect on trade include, but not limited to: (i) construction of timber processing plants in Mozambique to enable the export of logs; (ii) bilateral cooperation of coffee exports to upgrade the Ethiopian coffee industry; and (iii) bilateral cooperation on Sanitary and Phytosanitary measures (SPS) with various African countries (including South Africa and Kenya) to enable market access into China the various agricultural products from Africa, e.g., beef, lucerne, fresh and frozen fruits, flowers, beans, peanuts, maize seed, tobacco leaves, etc.

2.2.2. China's Bilateral Trade Agreements

Mutambara (2016:52) notes that in 2010, the People's Republic of China State Council announced that China had signed bilateral trade agreements with 45 African countries, and took initiatives to create favourable conditions for China-Africa trade development by enhancing cooperation in customs, taxation, inspection and quarantine. Furthermore, in order to give further support to African countries' export expansion into China, since 2005, China has offered zero tariffs on some of the exports originating from Least Developed Countries (LDCs) of Africa that have diplomatic relations with China. As a result, by July 2010, African products that enjoy zero-tariff treatment had increased to 47 000 taxable items, and were expected to cover 95% of the total taxable items mentioned in the Regulations of the People's Republic of China on Import and Export Duties. People's Republic of China State Council (2010) argues that because of the zero-tariff policy, exports of African products to China that entered duty-free grew rapidly. Thus, in the period 2005-2010, China had imported African products with an accumulated value of US $1.32 billion under zero-tariff terms, with such products including agricultural products, leather, stone materials, textiles and garments, machine spare parts, base metals and wood products.

2.2.3. China's Duty-Free Quota-Free (DFQF) Programme

To facilitate trade, trade development and economic development through trade with less developed countries (LDCs), China put in place a Duty-Free Quota-Free (DFQF) Programme, which is a non-reciprocal tariff preference treatment for LDCs launched on 1 July 2010. Through this

Programme, China seeks to open further its market to the LDCs by expanding the coverage of the Programme to 97 per cent of all tariff lines of China in the future. The scheme is accessible to all LDCs with diplomatic relations with China, and in 2011, notification of this preferential trade arrangement to benefit exporters from the LDCs was made with the World Trade Organisation, initially covering 30 African and 10 Southeast Asia countries (WTO Committee on Trade and Development, 2011a; 2011b). China's Duty-Free Quota-Free (DFQF) Programme was renewed in 2015, and currently 31 African countries[2] and 10 Southeast Asian countries are the beneficiary countries of China's preferential trade arrangement, as noted by Hu (2017) and WTO (2016:11). Viljoen (2019) notes that in 2018, the preferential market access granted was mostly duty free, except for certain products (411 tariff lines at HS10) which were levied MFN applied tariffs. While exports from outside beneficiary countries are supposed to enter the Chinese market at the MFN applied tariff rates, it has been observed that some of the imports sourced from China's major trading partners in Africa who are not beneficiary countries have been allowed entry into the Chinese market duty free. For example, South Africa is not a beneficiary country, and yet, as observed by Viljoen (2019:13), of the imports sourced from South Africa, 61% were imported into China duty-free.

2.2.4. Other Trade Facilitating Measures

Apart from offering duty free access into its market, China arguably gives further support for a general expansion of African countries exports to China by holding African commodity exhibitions, establishing African product exhibition centres and offering free stalls or reducing stall rents (Mutambara, 2016:52; People's Republic of China State Council, 2010).

---

[2] Angola, Benin, Burundi, Cambodia, Central African Republic, Chad, Comoros, Democratic Republic of the Congo, Djibouti, Equatorial Guinea, Eritrea, Ethiopia, Guinea, Guinea-Bissau, Lesotho, Liberia, Madagascar, Malawi, Mali, Mauritania, Mozambique, Niger, Rwanda, Senegal, Sierra Leone, Somalia, Sudan, Togo, Uganda, United Republic of Tanzania, Zambia (Hu, 2017; WTO, 2016:11).

3. METHODOLOGY, TECHNIQUES AND PROCEDURES

The trade data for empirical analysis necessary to evaluate and compare USA-Africa trade and China-Africa trade and its implications for industrial development for Africa, were obtained from the International Trade Centre trade database available at http://trademap.org and the UNCTAD trade data available at https://unctadstat.unctad.org/EN/. The indexes used for empirical evidence are: (i) the Intra-industry trade (β_i) index which shows the extent to which trading partners engage in two-way trade in goods with similar factor intensities. Intra-industry trade is important in high-value added manufactured goods which can be differentiated and benefit from economies of scale. Having intra-industry trade as a significant component of a country's trade has implications for technology transfer and developing the industrial base further; (ii) the revealed trade preference index (RTP_{ij}) is also known as the trade introversion index. The RTP_{ij} gives insights into whether the countries (or regions) regard each other as significant trading partners and the implications this has for strengthening and deepening trade ties; (iii) the trade complementarity indexes (TCI), which show how well the structure of a country's exports match (or complement) the import requirements of another country, as well as showing where trade relations could possibly be developed even further; and (iv) the revealed trade barrier (RTB_{ij}) indexes augmented by tariffs applied examine and compare ease of market access. Each of these indexes is discussed in the sections below.

3.1. Intra-Industry Trade Index

Intra-industry trade occurs when a country is *both* exporting and importing products in the same product classification category (goods of similar factor endowment or similar factor intensities). Over the years, this type of trade has become increasingly recognisable in international trade, and is becoming a significant part of trade, especially between developed economies because intra-industry trade will be relatively greater, compared to inter-industry trade, the more similar are the capital and labour endowments of countries being examined. However, as Mutambara (2017:104; 2013:23, 31; 2010:36, 37) note, some studies show that, although to some limited extent, intra-industry trade also occurs in trade between developed and developing countries as well as between developing countries. As Appleyard and Field (2017:193) observe, intra-industry trade is more important in manufactured goods than non-manufactured goods, and it is typically the highest for more sophisticated manufactured goods, as it is such goods that are more likely to benefit from economies of scale and are easier to differentiate, and thus facilitate trade in similar goods.

The intra-industry index developed by Grubel and Lloyd (1975) was used in this research to measure the potentials for intra-industry trade in product categories. While the Grubel and Lloyd (1975) empirical work was not the first application of the concept of intra-industry trade, it is the one most extensively used and as such became the focus of discussions about the implications of intra-industry trade results for trade theory. The Grubel-Lloyd (1975) intra-industry trade index is as follows:

$$\beta_i = 1 - \frac{|Xi - Mi|}{(Xi + Mi)} \tag{1}$$

where:

X_i = exports of product i;

M_i = imports of product i;

$(X_i + M_i)$ = total trade;

$|X_i - M_i|$ = the degree of non-overlap, i.e., the extent to which trade is unbalanced.

β_i = the intra-industry trade index, and it falls in the range $0 \leq \beta_i \leq 1$.

$\beta_i = 0$ indicates that trade flows just one way, thus no intra-industry trade.

$\beta_i = 1$ indicates perfect intra-industry trade, trade is balanced with exports equal imports.

Between these extremes, a high index indicates a greater degree of intra-industry trade. The intra-trade index can be converted into a percentage such that $0 \leq \beta_i \leq 100$ (Mutambara, 2017:99; 2013a:24).

Loertscher and Wolter (1980:282, 283) note the country hypotheses for intra-industry trade. They say that intra-industry trade among countries is intense if: (i) the average of their levels of development is high; (ii) the difference in their levels of development is relatively small; (iii) the average of their market size is large; (iv) the difference in their market sizes is small; and (v) barriers to trade are low. Thus, intra-industry trade intensity across countries increases with a decreasing development stage differential; a decreasing market size differential; increasing average market size; and decreasing distance between trading partner. Furthermore, Loertscher and Wolter (1980:284, 285) note that the industry hypotheses are that intra-industry trade in an industry is intense if: (i) the potential for product differentiation is high and market entry in narrow product lines is impeded by significant barriers; (ii) transaction costs are low; and (iii) the definition of an industry is comprehensive.

3.2. Bilateral Trade Intensity Index

Based on existing trade flows, trade intensity of bilateral trade indices are often used to measure the extent to which countries (or regions) trade with each other than with other countries (or regions). This gives some insights into whether the countries (or regions) regard each other as significant trading partners. The indices are used as indicators of the relative strength or resistance to bilateral trade flows. Thus, one would be able to infer that trade between two countries (or regions) is high not because these countries (or regions) are economically large (or small) but because the trade resistances between them are relatively low as noted by Bano (2014). Therefore, a trading partner tends to benefit more from trade with those partners it trades more intensively, as trade resistances are lower. The most widely used and well-known bilateral trade intensity index (I_{ij}) is given by the ratio between a partner country's (or region's) share of the reporting country's (or region's) total trade (Sij) and its share of world trade (W_j).

Thus, the bilateral trade intensity index is given by:

$$I_{ij} = (S_{ij})/(W_j) = (T_{ij}/T_{iw}))/(T_{Wj}/T_W) \quad (2)$$

where:

T_{ij} = trade (exports + imports) between reporting country i and partner country j;

T_{iW} = trade between the world and country i.

T_{Wj} = world trade with country j.

T_W = total world trade (Hamanaka, 2015:2; Iapadre and Tajoli, 2013:S93; Iapadre and Tiron, 2009:8).

However, as noted by Hamanaka (2015:4-5), Iapadre and Tajoli (2013:S93), Iapadre and Tiron (2009:7-10), Iapadre (2006:68-69), and Iapadre (2004:7-9); the bilateral trade intensity indices obtained using this formula (and its variations when it comes to the intra-regional trade index) have some limitations, *viz*. range variability, range asymmetry, and dynamic ambiguity. For the purpose of work done and presented in this chapter, all the three limitations are considered and corrected.

3.2.1. Correcting for Range Variability

This limitation must be corrected for because in this research, the indices computed are for different regions of different sizes and/or periods. In the traditional bilateral trade intensity index (I_{ij}), world trade (T_W) includes the reporting country's (or region's) trade. Therefore, as noted by Hamanaka (2015:4), if the country (or region) is large, this distorts the benchmark (world trade) as the benchmark includes that country (or region). This makes analysing the trend of a country (or region) whose weight in world trade is changing rapidly problematic. Furthermore, as noted by Hamanaka (2015:4), Iapadre and Tajoli (2013:S93), Iapadre and Tiron (2009:7-8) and Iapadre (2006:68), the range of the traditional bilateral trade intensity index is not homogeneous across regions. The range of the values of the index and the maximum value of the index depends on (or influenced by) the size of the partner country (or region). Therefore, the results of indices computed for different countries (or regions) and even over different periods are not perfectly comparable among each other.

The distortions to the benchmark (i.e., World trade) that arise from the size of the region are therefore corrected for by using "trade with *rest of the world*[3]" instead of "world trade" (T_W), thus taking care of the range variability, as the size of the region's trade is excluded from World trade (i.e., the benchmark). Therefore, the bilateral trade intensity index becomes the homogeneous bilateral trade intensity index (HI_{ij}), as its maximum value does not depend on the size of the partner country (or region). HI_{ij}, is given by the ratio between the partner country's (or region's) share of the reporting country's (or region's) total trade (Sij) and its weight in total trade of the *rest* of the world (Vij). In addition, trade intensity is a two-way measurement, e.g., country i's (or region i's) trade intensity towards country j (or region j), and country j's (or region j's) trade intensity toward country i (or region i). Region *i*'s homogeneous trade intensity towards region *j* is therefore given by

$$(HI_{ij}) = (S_{ij})/(V_{ij})$$
$$= (T_{ij}/T_i)/(T_{oj}/T_{ow}) \quad (3)$$

where:

T = total trade (exports + imports)

T_{ij} = exports of region *i* to region *j* + exports of region *j* to region *i* + imports of region *i* from region *j* + imports of region *j* from region *i* [i.e., trade between region *i* and region *j*]

T_i = total exports of region *i* to the world + total imports of region *i* from the world [i.e., trade between region *i* and the world]

T_{oj} = exports of world excluding region *i* (rest of the world) to region *j* + imports of world excluding region *i* (rest of the world) from region *j* [i.e., trade of region *j* with the rest of the world]

T_{ow} = total exports of world excluding region *i* + total imports of world excluding region *i* (Hamanaka, 2015:2; Iapadre and Tajoli, 2013:S93; Iapadre and Tiron, 2009:8).

HI_{ij} ranges between 0 (no bilateral trade) and ∞ (infinity) (only bilateral trade), i.e., $0 \leq (HI_{ij}) \leq \infty$. The maximum value is independent of the region's

[3] Rest of the world = World excluding country i (or region i).

trade size. $HI_{ij} = 1$ occurs when the importance of country j (or region j) for country i (or region i) is equal to its weight in world trade, i.e., a geographic neutrality threshold (Iapadre and Tajoli, 2013:S93; Iapadre and Tiron, 2009:8). Hamanaka (2015:4) notes that $HI_{ij} > 1$ means that a country (or region) has a positive bias toward the other country (or region). $HI_{ij} < 1$ means that a country (or region) has a negative bias toward the other country (or region).

3.2.2. Correcting for Range Symmetry and Dynamic Ambiguity

As noted by Hamanaka (2015:5), Iapadre and Tajoli (2013:S93), Iapadre (2006:69) and Iapadre (2004:8), the range symmetry problem arises from the fact that (HI_{ij}), is asymmetric around the geographic neutrality threshold of 1, as shown by $0 \leq (HI_{ij}) \leq \infty$. Thus, the range below 1 is smaller than the range above 1. Range asymmetry, as noted by Iapadre and Tajoli (2013:S93), Iapadre (2006:69) and Iapadre (2004:8), results in biased assessments of the index changes, depending on whether such changes occur above or below the geographic neutrality threshold. Furthermore, Iapadre and Tironi (2009:8) note that (HI_{ij}) is not bilaterally asymmetric as (HI_{ij}) is not necessarily equal to (HI_{ji}), unless the two partner countries (or regions) are equal.

Correcting for range asymmetry allows proper cross-regional comparisons of the results of the index. The range asymmetry problem is solved by standardising the index so as to obtain a symmetrical index of regional trade intensity given by $SI_{ij} = (HI_{ij} -1)/ (HI_{ij} +1)$. Thus, the range of the standardised transformation of the trade intensity index is $-1 \leq SI_{ij} \leq 1$, where $SI_{ij} = -1$ indicates no intra-regional (or inter-regional) trade, $SI_{ij} = 1$ indicates no extra-regional trade, and $SI_{ij} = 0$ indicates geographical neutrality (Iapadre, 2006:69; Iapadre, 2004:9). However, the symmetrical index of regional trade intensity is not exempt from the limitations that arise from dynamic ambiguity.

Hamanaka (2015:5) notes that dynamic ambiguity occurs when trade bias towards partner country X and the bias towards the rest of the world (world excluding partner country X) move in the same direction, thus a comovement problem. Iapadre (2006:70) notes that, "other things being equal, the probability of obtaining results that are dynamically ambiguous is higher when regional trade intensity is either very high or very low”.

Iapadre and Tajoli (2013:S94) and Iapadre (2004:9) note that when the comovement problem arises, this creates difficulties and confusion in interpreting the indices, as the indices will be conveying ambiguous information. In this case, trade intensity would be increasing (or decreasing) simultaneously with partner country X and with the rest of the world. What would have been expected is that when trade intensity increases (or decreases) with partner country X, trade intensity with the rest of the world (world excluding partner country X) should decrease (or increase). Therefore, as Iapadre (2006:70) and Iapadre (2004:14) argue, where there is a simultaneous increase (or fall) in both intra- and extra-regional trade intensity, any references that may need to be made regarding the effects of regional integration policies would be problematic, as the two indices would be contradicting each other.

3.3. Revealed Trade Preference Index (or Trade Introversion Index)

Both range asymmetry and dynamic ambiguity can be solved by considering the ratio between the difference and sum of the homogeneous intensity to a particular partner (HI_{ij}) and the homogeneous intensity to the rest of the world *excluding* the partner country (HE_{ij}). The extra-regional homogeneous *trade intensity* (HE_{ij}) between the regions is the complementary indicator for HI_{ij}, and it is calculated as follows:

$$(HE_{ij}) = (1\text{-}S_{ij})/(1\text{-}V_{ij})$$
$$= [1 - (T_{ij}/T_i)]/[1 - (T_{oj}/T_{ow})] \quad (4)$$

where T, T_{ij}, T_i, T_{oj}, and T_{ow} are defined as in Equation 3 above (Hamanaka, 2015:2; Iapadre and Tajoli, 2013:S93; Iapadre and Tiron, 2009:8).

The difference and sum of the homogeneous intensity of region *i* towards region *j* (HI_{ij}) and the homogeneous intensity to the rest of the world excluding region *j* (HE_{ij}) is the bilateral *revealed trade preference index* (RTP_{ij}) as noted by Iapadre and Tajoli (2013:8) and Iapadre and Tironi (2009:9). It is also regarded as region i's introversion towards region j, i.e., the trade introversion index, as noted by Hamanaka (2015:5) and Iapadre (2009:71). This index shows the relative bilateral trade intensity between the two regions, and the index is shown below.

$$RTP_{ij} = (HI_{ij} - HE_{ij})/(HI_{ij} + HE_{ij}) \quad (5)$$

where: $-1 \leq RTP_{ij} \leq +1$;

$RTP_{ij} = -1$ indicates no bilateral trade.

$RTP_{ij} = 1$ indicates only bilateral trade (or no extra-regional trade).

$RTP_{ij} = 0$ indicates geographic neutrality. Thus, the index ranges between -1 and +1, passing through the geographical neutrality of 0 (Hamanaka, 2015:2; Iapadre and Tajoli, 2013:8; Iapadre and Tironi, 2009:9).

Also to note is that the bilateral RTP, unlike all the other trade intensity indices, is perfectly symmetric, as $RTP_{ij} = RTP_{ji}$ independently of country size (Iapadre and Tajoli, 2013:8; Iapadre and Tironi, 2009:9; Iapadre, 2004:12). Since the bilateral *revealed trade preference index* (RTP_{ij}) is deemed robust and free of all the three limitations which the other trade intensity indexes face, the research presented in this chapter used this index to establish the inter-regional trade intensity between the USA and Africa, as well as China and Africa.

3.4. Revealed Trade Barrier Indices

Tariffs and non-tariff barriers are trade barriers and they both affect the ease with which products can access markets. Unlike tariff barriers, non-tariff barriers cannot be identified by simply examining the official tariff rates, and as such, revealed trade barriers (RTB) indexes are used to analyse a country's trade patterns to have insights into the ease of market access, and thus show whether goods from a particular source are possibly facing discriminatory or preferential treatment. Revealed trade barriers indexes seek to establish whether the imports by country, j, of a particular commodity, k, from country, i, are more or less important compared to country, j's total imports of that commodity from all sources. The indexes therefore serve as indicators of the possibilities of trade barriers against the importation of a commodity from a particular source (TIPS, 2019:6, Mutambara, 2016:55; Mutambara, 2017:99). The revealed trade barriers index is calculated as shown below.

$$RTB^j_{ik} = \frac{M^j_{ik} / \sum M^j_i}{\sum M_k / \sum M} \qquad (6)$$

where:

$M^j_{ik}/\Sigma M^j_i$ = the share of commodity k in country j imports from country i;

$\Sigma M_k / \Sigma M$ = the share of commodity k in world imports;

M^j_{ik} = imports of commodity k from country i by country j;

ΣM^j_i = total imports from country i by country j;

ΣM_k = total world imports of commodity k and

ΣM = total world imports

The results can be interpreted as follows:

If $0 \leq RTB^j_{ik} < 1$, then country i is exporting relatively more of commodity k to the rest of the world than to country j. Therefore, there is possibly discrimination against commodity k from country i into country j. If $RTB^j_{ik} = 1$, there is no discriminatory trade barrier against commodity k from country i in country j. If $RTB^j_{ik} > 1$, then country j is importing more from country i than expected. Therefore, there is possibly preferential treatment of commodity k from country i into country j (TIPS, 2019:6-7; Mutambara, 2016:55; Kalaba, et al., 2005:77).

It should, however, be noted that the RTB indexes serve as indicators that trade barriers exist but they do not specify the nature of these trade barriers. This shortcoming can be addressed by examining the specific non-tariff barriers to trade between countries as well as to examine tariffs the countries impose on each other's products.

3.5. Trade Complementarity Indices

Trade Complementarity Indices (TCI) provide useful information on the prospects for intra-regional (as well as inter-regional) trade by showing how well the structure of a country's exports match, or complement, the import requirements of another country. TCI therefore, approximate the adequacy of country j's export supply to country i's import demand by calculating the extent to which country i's total imports match country j's total exports. The trade complementarity index is given by the equation below.

$$TC_{ij} = 100\ [1 - \sum |Y_{ki} - X_{kj}|/2] \qquad (7)$$

where:

Y_{ki} is the share of good k in all imports of country i.

X_{kj} is the share of good k in all exports of country j.

$TC_{ij} = 0$ if there is no overlap at all.

$TC_{ij} = 100$ if imports and exports match perfectly (WITS, 2018; Vahalik, 2014:712; UNCTAD and WTO, 2012:30; Mikic and Gilbert, 2009:81).

The TCI can be used to determine the extent to which countries are natural trading partners in the sense that one country's imports overlap with another county's exports. Thus, it can be used to determine whether countries are well suited for prospective bilateral or regional trade agreements with each other. The TCI can be calculated from the perspective of each country to a trade agreement because while country i's import structure may not match country j's export structure, country j's import structure may match country i's export structure, thus indicating trade complementarity from country j's perspective. Analysing TCIs for a period of years, helps to determine whether countries' trade profiles were becoming more compatible. Furthermore, TCI can be used to see whether further development of trade relations would be economically beneficial for both countries.

In calculating the TCI between trading partners, it should be noted that the exports and imports are relative to the world and not to each other. This therefore leads to one of the shortcomings of the index. Therefore, as

Scholvin and Wrana (2015:8, 9) note, while the index may show a strong match between the trade profiles of countries, it does not say whether the amount supplied by one country satisfies the import demand of the other country, or alternatively whether the export amount is not too high to be absorbed by the importing country.

While the actual values of total exports and imports can be considered to establish whether one country's supply of the good can meet the other country's import demand for the good (despite the level of the TCI), it should be noted that some exports are ring-fenced for projects being carried out by other countries in the partner country. This is particularly so, for example, with regard to exports of mineral resources by some African countries where such exports are ring-fenced for infrastructure development by China. In such cases, high TCI levels, would not necessarily lead to an increase in trade between trading partners. Trade barriers negatively affect trade between countries because high trade barriers reduce the size of exports by one country to the other and thus reduce actual trade between the two countries despite high TCI levels. Furthermore, the level of aggregation of trade data affects the size of the TCI. The higher the level of trade aggregation is, the higher the TCI will be, thus masking the fact that some of the specific products within the broad product category may not match the import demand of such specific goods by the other country.

4. Results and Discussions

The trade data for empirical analysis necessary to evaluate and compare USA-Africa trade and China-Africa trade and its implications for industrial development for Africa, were obtained from the International Trade Centre trade database available at http://trademap.org, as well as the UNCTAD trade data available at http://unctadstat.org. The results for the indexes computed for empirical evidence as well as other information that show the nature of China-Africa trade and the USA-Africa trade are presented below.

4.1. Size of Trade with Africa

Table A-1 (Appendices) gives some insight into Africa's major trading partners as well as how China-Africa trade compares to USA-Africa trade. Africa's top ten trading partners are the USA, France, Italy, Germany, the United Kingdom, South Africa, Spain, China, India and the Netherlands. The USA was Africa's largest trading partner in 2001-2008, after which in 2009, China became Africa's number one trade partner for the first time. Thus, in the period 2009-2019, China superseded the USA to be Africa's largest trading partner. Therefore, as the global economy recovered after the global financial crisis, China-Africa trade also maintained a favourable recovery and development momentum. In 2020, China ranked as Africa's largest trading partner, with China-Africa trade contributing 48.6% to Africa's total world trade. The USA became Africa's third largest trading partner after France, with USA-Africa trade constituting 12.4% of Africa's total trade, while France-Africa trade constituting 13.6% of Africa's total trade. Germany and Spain ranked 4th and 5th respectively, where their trade with Africa contributed 11.0% and 10.4% to Africa's total trade, respectively.

China-Africa trade rose from US $8.2 billion in 2001 to US $170 billion in 2019, after which it fell drastically to US $51.8 billion in 2020. From 2001, China-Africa trade rose continuously up to 2013, after which it fell continuously to 2016, and then rose again to 2019. Significantly large China-Africa trade was experienced in 2010-2019, with trade rising from US$112 billion to US $170 billion in that period. The USA-Africa trade rose from US $31.8 billion in 2001 to US $53.3 billion in 2019, after which it fell to US $22.5 billion in 2020. USA-Africa trade was on a continuous rise in 2001-2008; and experienced a continuous fall in 2012-2015 after which it recovered. Significantly large USA-Africa trade were experienced in 2007, 2008, 2010 and 2011, with trade ranging between US $101 billion and US $131 billion.

The USA-Africa trade generated a trade surplus for Africa in 2001-2013, while China-Africa trade generated a trade deficit for Africa, for most years, except 2007, 2008, 2011 and 2012. In this regard therefore, the claim by People's Republic of China State Council (2010) that for years, China has been promoting comprehensive and balanced trade with Africa; is not correct. Instead, it is the USA that has been promoting balanced and favourable trade with Africa, as for most years Africa enjoyed trade surpluses in its trade with the USA.

4.2. Major Trading Partners in Africa

The results for trade with specific African countries show that for both the USA and China, their major trading partners in Africa are South Africa, Nigeria, Angola, Egypt and Algeria, as shown in Tables A-2 and A-3 (Appendices). These five countries contributed 50% - 63% of China's total trade with Africa, with the highest contributions of 60%-63% in the period 2011-2014. For the USA, these five countries jointly contributed 61% - 79% of the USA's total trade with Africa, with the highest contributions of 72%-79% experienced in the period 2001-2012. These five countries are some of Africa's countries that are well-endowed with large mineral and oil reserves. It is a common phenomenon and characteristic of African countries that have large mineral and oil reserves that such countries have gained favourable trade relations with both China and the USA.

4.2.1. Algeria

Algeria is North Africa's largest economy and an important gas- and oil-exporting country. Hamaizia (2020) notes that the China-Algeria trade and investment relations took off in earnest in the 2000s, and that from China's perspective, there are four key drivers to the relationship, *viz.* (i) Algeria's geostrategic location with proximity to Europe and access to the Sahel and the Sub-Saharan region – for example through the Trans-Saharan Highway – making it an important hub for the Belt and Road Initiative; (ii) Algeria's political influence in the Mediterranean and in the African Union; (iii) Algeria as a key arena for government contracts and commercial opportunity for Chinese companies; and (iv) Algeria's latest mining plans for mining phosphates, gold, uranium, zinc and iron ore, provide new opportunities for

China's perpetual pursuit of raw materials. Hamaizia (2020) and Calabrese (2021) note that initiatives which have helped to deepen and strengthen trade and economic relations between the two countries include the Forum on China-Africa Cooperation (FOCAC), China-Arab States Cooperation Forum (CASCF), as well as the Comprehensive Strategic Partnership which is the highest tier of diplomatic and economic relations which China affords to its most important partners. The 2018 Memorandum of Understanding on cooperation under the Belt and Road Initiative framework would also strengthen relations between the two countries.

Table A-2 (Appendices) shows that Algeria is China's 5th largest trading partner in Africa, with China-Algeria trade rising from US $0.29 billion in 2001 to US $8.09 billion in 2019. Trade between the two countries has been on a general upward trend, peaking at US $9.10 billion in 2018. China-Algeria trade has always resulted in a trade deficit for Algeria, with this deficit on a continuous increase, rising from US $0.2 billion in 2001 to US $5.8 billion in 2019, and peaking at US $7.4 billion in 2016.

The USA regards Algeria as a strategically located and capable partner with which it has strong diplomatic relations. Among other things, growing economic and commercial links is one of the primary objectives of the USA engagement with Algeria. In July 2001, the two countries signed a Trade and Investment Framework Agreement (TIFA) that provides a platform to address impediments in the economic relationship and identify paths to broader commercial interaction (US Department of State, 2021a; US Embassy in Algeria, 2017; Zoubir, 2011). Zoubir (2011) notes that a bilateral treaty on investment, trade benefits and taxation emerged from the TIFA and the objective of the agreement was to double the volume of trade between the two countries and allow American companies to get a larger share of the Algerian market, particularly in the oil sector. As such as noted by US Department of State (2021a), US Embassy in Algeria (2017), and Zoubir (2011), the hydrocarbon sector is significant to most USA direct investment in Algeria, and the United States is currently the largest investor in this sector and its investments outside the oil sector remain insignificant. In March 2004, Algeria was designated as eligible for the Generalised System of Preferences.

Economic relations between Algeria and the United States have expanded significantly and bilateral trade between the two countries has grown steadily. Table A-3 (Appendices) shows that in 2001-2014, Algeria mainly ranked 2nd or 3rd among the USA's trading partners in Africa, and since 2017, it has ranked 4th. USA-Algeria trade rose from US $3.74 billion in 2001 peaking at US $21.3 billion in 2008, after which it dropped drastically to US$12.3billion in 2009. While it recovered in the next two years, it dropped again in 2012 and remained in a downward trajectory to US $3.59 billion in 2019. The USA-Algeria trade has always yielded a trade surplus for Algeria, with significantly high trade surpluses experienced in 2005-2012 where this ranged between US $8.84 billion and US $18.8 billion. After 2012, the trade surplus was on a general decline, falling from US $8.84 billion in 2012 to US $1.59 billion in 2019.

4.2.2. Angola

Angola is the second largest oil producer in Africa, and in January 2007, Angola formally joined the Organisation of Petroleum Exporting Countries (OPEC), underlining its growing role in the global energy system. Apart from trade activities, China's non-trade activities in Angola such as aid, loans, and foreign direct investments are mainly concentrated in oil and resource extraction areas. Table A-2 (Appendices) shows that Angola is China's second largest trading partner in Africa, after South Africa. China-Angola trade rose from US $0.77 billion in 2001 to US $25.4 billion in 2019, with 2006 marking the beginning of a significant rise in China- Angola trade. Trade between China and Angola always yielded a positive trade balance in favour of Angola, with such a trade surplus rising from US $0.68 billion in 2001 to US $21.3 billion in 2019.

As Africa's second largest oil producer, it has been argued that USA economic policy for Angola is deeply rooted in protecting the stability of its oil and energy supply. Malaquias (2011:12) argues that Angola's importance as a trade partner to the USA increased dramatically with the rise of oil as a dominant commodity to Angola's economy. Table A-3 (Appendices) shows that Angola is the USA's fifth largest trading partner in Africa and USA-Angola trade rose from US $3.37 billion in 2001 to its highest of US $21.6

billion in 2008. After 2011, trade between the two countries was on a continuous decline, falling from US $15.3 billion in 2011 to US $1.52 billion in 2019. The USA-Angola trade always maintained a trade surplus in favour of Angola, with such a trade surplus on a continuous rise in the period 2001-2008. According to Malaquias (201114, 15), Angola became a beneficiary of AGOA in 2003 and signed a Trade and Investment Framework and Agreement (TIFA) in 2009 to facilitate further investment and bilateral trade with the USA. In 2010, the US-Angola Strategic Partnership Dialogue Agreement was signed to formalise increased bilateral partnerships in, among other things, energy, security and trade. Tralac (2015) states that more than four thousand Angolan products, particularly oil and its derivatives, also receive exemption of customs duties under the GSP and MFN tariffs.

4.2.3. Egypt

Egypt was the first Arab and African country to establish direct diplomatic relations with China in 1956. In the decades that followed, the relationship and the bilateral cooperation have endured, grown and remained positive (Dahshan, 2021; Badri, 2020; Gadallah, 2016; Tiezzi, 2015; Hatab, 2012). Consequently, different agreements and protocols have been signed between the two countries, especially in the economic and commercial spheres. Since then, there have been several trade exchanges between the two countries, such that the trade volume between the two countries has been rising (Gadallah, 2016). A significant turning point in China-Egypt relations came in 2014, with the signing of the Comprehensive Strategic Partnership (CSP) by the two countries. Since then, China and Egypt have signed at least 25 bilateral agreements (Dahshan, 2021; Badri, 2020; Tiezzi, 2015). Furthermore, the China-Africa Cooperation Forum has served to deepen strategic partnership between the two sides. Table A-2 (Appendices) shows that Egypt ranks 4th among China's trading partners in Africa, and China-Egypt trade was on a gradual increase from US $0.95 in 2001 to US $13.2 in 2019. Much higher trade was experienced from 2013 onwards with such trade ranging between US $10.2 billion and US $13.9 billion. China-Egypt trade always posted a trade surplus in favour of China, with Egypt's trade deficit in its trade with China worsening from US $0.8 billion in 2001 to US $11 billion in 2019.

The United States established diplomatic relations with Egypt in 1922. Under the Qualifying Industrial Zone Agreement, the United States waives duties on imports from Egypt if the value includes 10.5% Israeli content, a programme which seeks to promote stronger ties between the region's peace partners (US Department of State, 2021b). Egypt and the United States signed a Trade and Investment Framework Agreement in 1999 to serve as a step toward creating freer trade and increasing investment flows (US Department of State, 2021b; American Chamber of Commerce in Egypt, 2020). Furthermore, American Chamber of Commerce in Egypt (2020) notes that there are two initiatives designed to increase Egypt's exports to the USA, *viz*. (i) the USA Generalised System of Preferences (GSP); and (ii) the Qualifying Industrial Zones (QIZs), which is a one-way free trade arrangement (FTA) that combines Egyptian and Israeli components in manufactured goods from designated industrial zones that enter the USA duty-free. In December 2017, a bilateral Trade and Investment Council was convened to discuss ways to further expand economic activity between the two countries. Due to the initiatives to boost USA-Egypt relations, US Department of State (2021) notes that American firms are active in most sectors of the Egyptian economy, including oil and gas exploration and production, financial services, manufacturing, construction, telecommunications and information technology, and the restaurant and hospitality industry. While the USA-Egypt Free Trade Agreement negotiations are yet to resume, Mabrouk (2019) and Broadbent (2011) argue that there are strong economic and trade policy reasons for pursuing such an arrangement as it would benefit US companies which are currently at a disadvantage *vis-à-vis* competing companies in Europe due to the EU-Egypt Association Agreement. Table A-3 (Appendices) shows that Egypt's position as the USA trading partner in Africa improved greatly over the years, rising from ranking 5th in 2003-2012 to ranking mainly 3rd after that. The USA-Egypt trade rose gradually from US $4.44 billion in 2001 to US $8.78 billion in 2019. Among the USA's top five major trading partners in Africa, Egypt is the only one with which the USA always experienced a trade surplus. Egypt's trade deficit with the USA was highest in 2008-2015, ranging between US $3.1 billion and US $5.0 billion.

4.2.4. Nigeria

While the economic relations between China and Nigeria can be traced back to 1971, Ajayi (2020) states that current relations and the growth of bilateral trade between Nigeria and China were strengthened and boosted by the establishment of FOCAC in 2000 and the Beijing Conference in 2006. Table A-2 (Appendices) shows that Nigeria is China's third largest trading partner in Africa, with the China-Nigeria trade rising from US $1.14 billion in 2001 to US $19.3 billion in 2019. A significant increase in China-Nigeria trade occurred after 2010, with trade ranging between US $10.8 billion and US $19.3 billion in the period 2011-2019. China-Nigeria trade always posted a trade surplus in favour of China, and Nigeria's trade deficit with China on a continuous rise from US $0.7 billion in 2001 to US $14 billion in 2019.

Table A-3 (Appendices) shows that Nigeria was the USA's leading African trade partner until 2013, after which South Africa overtook Nigeria to rank 1st as USA's trading partner in Africa. 2005-2012 saw very high USA-Nigeria trade, with such trade ranging between US $24.4 billion and US $43.3 billion in that period. Except for 2014 and 2015, the USA-Nigeria trade yielded positive trade balances in favour of Nigeria, with the trade surplus rising continuously from US$7.82billion in 2001 to peak at US $35.1 billion in 2008. Saidi (2002, in Mba, 2013) notes that, among other things, addressing human rights violations and making meaningful progress in transitioning into a democratic state, helped Nigeria to become eligible for AGOA. Thus, the AGOA programme has helped to diversify and broaden Nigeria's non-oil exports to the USA, which were 90 per cent oil before AGOA. Adam (2012, in Mba, 2013) argues that the USA economic policies towards Nigeria are helping Nigeria achieve sustainable growth by opening markets for its exports, reducing barriers to investment and identifying opportunities and areas of comparative advantages.

4.2.5. South Africa

South Africa ranks 1st among China's trading partners in Africa, while China became South Africa's number one trading partner after 2010. Alden and Wu (2014) note that South Africa granted China market economy status in 2004 as part of their strategic partnership, in order to "narrow the parameters to pursue certain kinds of trade disputes in terms of World Trade Organization (WTO) criteria." The admittance of South Africa as a member of BRICS[4] in December 2010 has helped to enhance China-South Africa trade relations since multilateral schemes/ arrangements generate fair gains for the participating countries. Such gains or advantages are said to relate to, among other things, trade and market access, as such schemes increases the chances of a member country to establish free trade/or easy trade with the other BRICS member countries. Table A-2 (Appendices) shows that South Africa has already witnessed high trade volume increase with China. China-South Africa trade rose from US $2.22 billion in 2001 to US $42.5 billion in 2019. Significantly high trade between the two countries was observed in 2012-2014 with their trade ranging between US$60billion and US $65.2 billion in that period. From 2008, China-South Africa trade always posted positive trade balances in favour of South Africa with the trade surplus rising from US $0.62 billion in 2008 to US $9.37 billion in 2019. Very high trade surpluses of between US$28.9billion and US $31.6 billion were experienced in the period 2012-2014.

Table A-3 (Appendices) shows that since 2014, South Africa has ranked 1st among the USA trading partners in Africa, thus overtaking Nigeria. USA-South Africa trade rose from US $7.39 billion in 2001 to US $13.3 billion in 2019. USA-South Africa trade always posted trade surpluses in favour of South Africa, with such the surplus rising from US$1.47 in 2001 to US $2.65 in 2019. South Africa is a beneficiary of AGOA, and this gives South African goods trade preferences into the USA market. Cook (2020:27, 28) ranks South Africa as the largest non-oil exporting AGOA beneficiary and

---

[4] BRICS is a multilateral arrangement of five countries, i.e., Brazil, Russia, India, China and South Africa, and these countries constituted 42% of the world's population by 2017. China is the biggest of the five countries, constituting 67% of the five countries' GDP by 2016 (Statistics South Africa, 2018).

the second largest beneficiary overall. In 2012, South Africa and the USA signed a Trade and Investment Framework Agreement (TIFA), which facilitates investment and bilateral trade between the two countries, and South Africa also benefits under the GSP (Cook, 2020:27; Mutambara, 2017:105). Cook (2020:29) states that over the past decade, 14% under GSP and 23% under AGOA of South African products have been exported to the USA duty-free.

4.2.6. Concluding Comments

Over the years, both China and the USA have been increasing the value of their trade with each of the five countries. China's trade with these countries (except for Angola and during the last 12 years of its trade with South Africa) has resulted in trade deficits for these countries, with the trade deficits worsening over the years. On the contrary, USA trade with these countries (except Egypt) has yielded trade surpluses in favour of the Africa countries. Therefore, USA trade with these countries has benefitted the countries more than their trade with China, given that a trade balance is the largest component of the current account, which is itself the largest component of the balance of payments. Most low income and developing countries try to avoid a trade deficit, unless the trade deficit arises due to importing capital equipment and components that they cannot produce themselves.

The steady growth in the countries' trade deficits with China over the years has most likely eliminated some jobs in those sectors which are the major sources for the trade deficits. Loss of jobs in sectors that are the major sources of the trade deficit, not only has implications for the unemployment rate, but also affects the composition of employment. The workers who are no longer employed in those sector find jobs elsewhere in the long run, usually in industries where wages are much lower. This thus has implications for dramatically increasing the level of income inequality in the society. Unemployment levels and income inequalities are already at unacceptable high levels in African countries and so, these unwelcome potential effects of trade deficits serve to exacerbate these problems.

Increased imports from China, leading to the huge trade deficits currently experienced by the African countries in their trade with China, can also have displacement effects, as African producers might not be able to compete with their Chinese counterparts. This applies in particular to specific labour-intensive manufactured goods, such as textiles, footwear or furniture, where African producers have had a considerable market share in local markets, but find themselves being crowded out by Chinese imports in the local market. Such import penetration negatively affects the manufacturing sector and may constrain/or prevent African countries from diversifying their own industry.

Since China has emerged to be the major trading partner for African countries, the ever increasing and high levels of trade deficit the countries experience in trading with China, worsens these countries overall annual trade deficits as a trade deficit with China alone is a significant component of their overall annual trade deficit. Furthermore, trade deficits result in capital outflows to finance these deficits, money that African countries do not have due to their lower levels of industrial development. As a result, they often resort to using foreign capital inflows to finance these deficits, thus further pushing them into debt. While volume restrictions may be set to reduce the trade deficit, this may however constrain entry of essential inputs needed by local producer, which may result in raising production costs.

The recurring and rising trade surplus the African countries enjoy in their trade with the USA has positive implications for these countries. High and increased exports from the sectors which are the major sources for the trade surplus lead to increased employment and better jobs in these export sectors. Increased foreign demand for products produced in these sectors would also motivate countries to develop and modernise these sectors more in an effort to meet foreign demand. Furthermore, trade surpluses that arise from trade with the USA through increased exports contribute towards improvements in a country's overall trade balance, which in turn can increase income and hence raise national savings, if the overall outcome is a positive trade balance.

4.3. China versus USA as Imports Sources and Exports Destinations for the Countries

This section discusses, examines and compares the extent to which China and the USA are exports destinations and sources of imports for the top five African countries they trade with, and the results presented in Table A-4 (Appendices) are used. The extent to which trade with China and the USA contribute to the five countries total world trade is also examined using the results presented in Table A-5 (Appendices). While it is merely the size of trade in terms of value that is used, this is helpful in giving some basic insights into the extent to which China and the USA are important trading partners to the Africa countries. A more comprehensive analysis of the extent to which both China and the USA trade intensively with each of the five countries (i.e., trade orientation), will be presented in Section 4.5 below.

4.3.1. Algeria

The European Union (especially France, Italy, Germany, Spain, and Turkey) has always been Algeria's major source for its imports[5]. Table A-4 (Appendices) shows that China emerged to rank 3rd as an imports source in 2005, and proceeded to rank 2nd in 2009-2012. Since 2013, it has ranked 1st as Algeria's major imports source. The USA's position as an imports source has mainly been between 6th and 7th position. However, China has never appeared among Algeria's top ten exports destinations, while the USA ranked 1st in the period 2001-2011, after which it fell to rank 4th in the period 2013-2017. In this regard therefore, China plays the role of a source for imports while the USA plays that of an exports' destination.

Table A-5 (Appendices) shows that the contribution of China-Algeria trade to Algeria's total world trade has seen a continuous increase over the years, rising from 0.97% in 2001 to 11.1% by 2017. USA-Algeria trade's share in Algeria's world trade was on a steady increase from 12.7% in 2001 to 23.0% in 2007, after which it was on a downward trajectory to a level of

[5] See Algeria's major trading partners from the trade data reported by Algeria and available in the International Trade Centre trade database available at http://www.trademap.org.

6.54% in 2019. Therefore, while throughout the years China managed to sustain the increase in its share in Algeria's total trade, the USA was not been able to do so after 2007.

4.3.2. Angola

Portugal has always been Angola's major source for imports and has ranked 1st as Angola's imports source for many years[6]. Table A-4 (Appendices) shows that China emerged to rank 2nd after Portugal in 2009-2017, and overtook Portugal to rank 1st in 2018 and 2019. In 2004-2007, the USA ranked 2nd as Angola's imports source, after which it mainly ranked 3rd for the rest of the period, falling to 6th position in 2019. Since 2007, China has ranked 1st as Angola's exports destination while for the USA, its position shifted between 2nd, 3rd and 4th. While both China and the USA rank favourably as sources of imports as well as destinations for exports, these roles have mainly been taken by China than by the USA.

Table A-5 (Appendices) shows that China-Angola trade has had a significant big share in Angola's world trade. The share of this trade in Angola's total world trade rose from a mere 3.49% in 2004 to 47.8% in 2019, with shares of 30.0% - 47.8% experienced from 2010 onwards. The share of USA-Angola trade in Angola's world trade was generally on an increase rising from 7.95% in 2005 to 20.9% in 2011, after which there was a steady decline to 3.24% by 2019. China's trade with Angola thus plays a much bigger role in Angola's world trade than the USA's trade with Angola. While the share of USA-Angola trade in Angola's world trade was declining, the share of China-Angola trade in Angola's world trade was rising significantly.

4.3.3. Egypt

Table A-4 (Appendices) shows that the USA ranked 1st as Egypt's imports source in 2001-2011, after which it dropped to rank mainly 3rd. In 2001-2007, China ranked mainly 3rd as an imports source, after which it rose to rank 2nd after the USA, and eventually overtaking the USA to rank 1st

---

[6] See Angola's major trading partners from the trade data reported by Angola and available in the International Trade Centre trade database available at http://www.trademap.org.

from 2012 onwards. As an exports destination, China never appeared among Egypt top ten exports destinations. Italy has always been Egypt's top exports destination[7], with the USA ranking either 2nd or 3rd in 2001-2012, after which its position declined to mainly 5th. In 2019, the USA rose to rank 1st as Egypt's exports destination, thus overtaking Italy. Therefore, between the two countries, the USA has played the role of an exports destination. At different times, both China and the USA have been significant sources of imports for Egypt, with the USA playing that role in a more significant way before China became the second largest world economy. After China became the second largest world economy in 2010, it took over from the USA the role of Egypt's top major source for its imports.

Table A-5 (Appendices) shows that China-Egypt trade as a share of Egypt's total world trade has been on a steady increase over the years, from 3.28% in 2001 to 11.5% in 2019. On the other hand, the share of USA-Egypt trade in Egypt's world trade has been steadily declining, from 12.9% in 2001 to 6.80% in 2019.

4.3.4. Nigeria

Table A-4 (Appendices) shows that in the period 2006-2011, China and the USA alternated to rank 1st and 2nd as sources for Nigeria's imports. From 2012, China consistently ranked 1st as Nigeria's imports source, with the USA consistently ranking 2nd until 2018 and 2019 when its position fell to 4th. The USA ranked 1st as Nigeria's exports destination in the period 2001-2012, after which it was superseded by India. China has tended to rank mainly as Nigeria's 10th exports destination. While both China and the USA have proved to be significant sources for imports for Nigeria, the USA has been an important destination for Nigeria's exports.

Table A-5 (Appendices) shows that the share of China-Nigeria trade in Nigeria's total world trade has generally been on an upward trajectory, rising from 2.51% in 2001 to 13.6% in 2019. USA-Nigeria trade contributed significantly to Nigeria's world trade in 2001-2008 where this trade constituted 25.4% - 36.8% of Nigeria's total trade. After 2011, this share fell

[7] See Egypt's major trading partners from the trade data reported by Egypt and available in the International Trade Centre trade database available at http://www.trademap.org.

significantly and by 2019, the USA-Angola contributed 7.43% of Angola's world trade.

4.3.5. South Africa

Table A-4 (Appendices) shows that the USA has always ranked 3rd as South Africa's imports source, with China ascending to rank 2nd in 2005 and eventually ranking 1st from 2008 onwards, thus overtaking Germany[8] which had always ranked 1st as a source of imports for South Africa, and now ranking 2nd. The USA ranked 1st as a destination for South Africa's exports in the period 2001-2008, after which it fell to rank 2nd, a position it held until 2017, after which it fell to 3rd position in 2018 and 2019. China emerged to rank 1st in 2009, and continued to hold that position for the rest of the period. While both countries have been important sources of imports and destinations for South Africa exports, over the years, China strengthened its role as both a source for imports and a destination for South Africa's exports.

Table A-5 (Appendices) shows that the share of China-South Africa trade in South Africa's total trade has been on a constant increase, rising from 2.96% in 2001 to 14.5% in 2019. High trade shares were experienced from 2009 when China became South Africa's top trading partner. USA-South Africa's trade shares in South Africa's total trade were on a consistent gentle decline, from 12.9% in 2001 to 6.77% in 2019.

4.3.6. Concluding Comments

Since opening up to foreign trade and investment as well as implementing free-market reforms in 1979, China proceeded to join the World Trade Organisation (WTO) in December 2001. China's entry into the WTO helped it to cement its status as the world's factory and largest trader. Its participation in Africa's trade has as a result also grown significantly, as evidenced by its ascendance to rank 1st as a more favourably source of imports by the African countries, compared to the USA. China's growing global economic influence and the economic and trade policies it maintains

---

[8] See South Africa's major trading partners from the trade data reported by South Africa and available in the International Trade Centre trade database available at http://www.trademap.org.

with African countries are being translated into China's rising trade shares in the African countries' world trade. This has significant implications for the role of the United States as a trading partner for Africa, and the continuous decline in the USA trade shares in the African countries total trade implies reduced USA trade orientation towards Africa. Therefore, between the two countries, the value of China's trade with the African countries has been improving over the years compared to that of the USA. In 2010, China overtook Japan to become the world's second largest economic powerhouse, behind the USA, in terms of GDP expressed in current prices or nominal terms. Its growth has also enabled it to be a stronger competitor to the USA with regard to accessing more lucrative trade with African countries. Furthermore, China's policy of non-interference in partner countries' domestic affairs serves as an advantage over the USA who bundle their economic and other agreements with demands for democratisation and human rights protection. The vast Chinese market provides wide space for African products, while China's continued rapid economic growth has created a stable export market for Africa's resource products.

4.4. Types of Products Traded

As per the Heckscher-Ohlin theorem[9], different relative factor endowments between countries have implications for trade between countries. Thus, the country with abundant capital will be able to produce relatively more of the capital-intensive good, while the country with abundant labour will be able to produce relatively more of the labour-intensive good. Therefore, a country will export the commodity that uses relatively more intensively its relatively abundant factor of production, and it will import the good that uses relatively intensively its relatively scarce factor of production (Appleyard and Field, 2017:128, 132; Eisenman,

[9] The underlining key assumptions are identical technology in both countries, constant returns to scale, and a given factor-intensity relationship between final goods (Appleyard and Field, 2017:124; Subasat, 2003:150).

2012:797, 798; Subasat, 2003:150). African countries are resource abundant countries[10], and as such, they tend to be able to produce relatively more of the resource-intensive goods, and thus mainly export those commodities that use relatively more intensively their relatively abundant factors of production, which are resources.

4.4.1. Types of Major Imports from Africa by Both China and the USA

Tables A-6 (Appendices) shows that for both the USA and China, Mineral fuels, Non-fuel primary commodities, and Resource–intensive manufactured goods dominate their top 20 major imports from Africa. There are very few high value added manufactured products. In the period 2001-2019, Table A-7 (Appendices) shows that the top 20 products imported from Africa constituted 85.3% - 98.1% of the USA's total imports from Africa, while Tables A-8 (Appendices) shows that the top 20 products imported from Africa constituted 93.2% - 98.8% of China's total imports from Africa.

Tables A-7 and A-8 (Appendices) show that for both the USA and China, the single major import from Africa is HS27 (Mineral fuels) which is a product category made up of Coal, coke and briquettes; Petroleum, petroleum products and related materials; Gas, natural and manufactured; and Electric current (Electrical energy). Table A-7 (Appendices) show that for the USA, HS27 (Mineral fuels) contributed 73.7% - 85.8% of USA total imports from Africa in 2001-2012, after which that share fell continuously to 40.27% by 2019. Table A-8 (Appendices) shows that in 2001-2019, HS27 (Mineral fuels) contributed 58.3% - 82.3% of China's total imports from Africa. This is consistent with arguments that China's energy needs and energy security agenda is a priority. Therefore, as Mutambara (2016:57) noted, Africa, just as Brazil, Australia, and the Russian Federation, are significant mineral fuels import sources for China. The Mineral fuels, Non-fuel primary commodities, and Resource–intensive manufactured goods in the top 20 imports from Africa jointly constituted 70.4% - 95.3% of the USA's total imports from Africa and 92.3% - 98.2% of China's total imports

[10] Abundant in mineral resources, land for agriculture, forestry and fisheries, as well as labour, especially unskilled, low skilled and medium skilled labour.

from Africa. Africa is a resource-rich Continent, and as per the Heckscher-Ohlin theorem[11], would logically have most of its exports originating from the mining and agricultural sectors.

Therefore, for both the USA and China, Africa continues to serve mainly as a supplier/or source for raw materials and low-value added inputs. China and USA are very big markets for Africa and the nature of their major imports from Africa thus tend to confine Africa to its areas of comparative advantages in low value added products. Comparative advantage is endogenously determined by past technological change, and therefore, specialisation according to current comparative advantage under free trade may be welfare reducing for the African countries. Thus, being confined to these areas of comparative advantages does not work towards Africa's focus/goals in developing its economy further through developing a more robust manufacturing sector.

Table A-6 (Appendices) shows that among the top 20 imports by both the USA and China are also a few High skill technology intensive manufactured goods, and Medium skill technology intensive manufactured goods which are in the form of Transport and equipment, Chemicals and Polymers, Machinery, Electrics and Electronics. Tables A-7 (Appendices) shows that these constitute 2.7% - 6.8% of the USA's top 20 imports from Africa in the period 2001-2012, after which the share rose to 7.9% - 14.9% for 2013-2019. Compared to the USA, Table A-8 (Appendices) shows that China had even fewer High- and Medium-skill technology-intensive manufactured goods in its top 20 imports from Africa, with such products contributing an even lower share of 0.3% - 2.3% of the total value of the top 20 imports from Africa.

Tables A-7 and A-8 (Appendices) also show the import shares of all products classified as High-skill and technology-intensive manufactures[12] and those classified as Medium-skill and technology-intensive

---

[11] A neoclassical trade theory based on the principle of comparative advantage where, given all the products that could be produced; a country focusses on producing a commodity it can produce at a lower opportunity cost compared to the other country (Leamer, 1995; Subasat, 2003; Appleyard and Field, 2017).

[12] These manufactured products are found in product categories HS28 – HS39; very few HS84; HS85; HS88; HS90 and HS91.

manufactures[13], in China and the USA total imports from Africa. For the USA, the High-skill and technology-intensive manufactures it imported from Africa contributed 2.1% of its total imports from Africa in 2001, rising to 7.4% by 2019. The Medium-skill and technology-intensive manufactures contributed 2.5% in 2001 rising to peek at 7.2% in 2015. Jointly, these two groups of high value-added manufactured products had an import share of 4.6% in 2001, which rose to 11.8% by 2019. The import shares of such products in China's total imports from Africa were much lower, e.g., the import share of High-skill and technology-intensive manufactures was 4.1% in 2001 and fell continuously to 1.0% by 2019. The same pattern is observed with regard to the Medium-skill and technology-intensive manufactures imported, with their share in total imports from Africa falling continuously from 2.2% in 2001 to 0.5% by 2019. Jointly, these two groups of high value-added manufactured products had an import share of 6.3% in 2001 and declined continuously to 1.5% by 2019. Therefore, while the USA increased the import share of high value-added manufactured goods in its imports from Africa, China was doing the opposite; i.e., decreasing the import share of high value added manufactured goods in its imports from Africa.

Therefore, the USA is taking more meaningful and effective initiatives to building effective demand in its economy for Africa's high value-added manufactured exports. It allows in such goods by ensuring that these products contribute a reasonably high share of its imports from Africa. Africa, just like any developing economies, faces a trade-off between specialising according to existing comparative advantage (in resource-intensive and low-technology goods) and entering sectors in which they currently lack a comparative advantage but may acquire such an advantage in the future as a result of the potential for productivity growth in high-technology goods. Therefore, where big markets take deliberate initiatives to import more high value-added manufactured goods from developing countries (as the USA is doing with regard to Africa), this would be welfare improving for both trading partners. Furthermore, it helps the less developed trading partner to utilise more fully its past technological capabilities while

[13] These manufactured products are found in product categories HS40, few HS39; HS84; few HS85; and HS87.

simultaneously shaping and improving current rates of innovation and absorbing new technologies. In this regard, the USA-Africa trade is demonstrating this more than the China-Africa trade.

Currently, the contribution of High- and Medium-skill technology-intensive manufactured goods is small in both China and USA import baskets. However, the presence of such high manufactured value-added products from Africa in both China and USA import baskets, reflects initiatives by African countries to modernise and strengthen their industrial bases in order to have a level of industrial complexity in the Continent's manufacturing sector, such that high value-added manufactured products can compete in international markets.

Table A-9 (Appendices) show that the major imports by both the USA and China from their five major trading partners in Africa tend to mirror that of imports from Africa in general. With regard to Algeria, Angola and Nigeria, HS27 (Mineral fuels) constituted the largest share of China and the USA's total imports from these countries. For China, HS27 (Mineral fuels) constituted 73.4% - 99.6% of China's total imports from Algeria, while for the USA, 95.0% - 99.9% of total imports from Algeria were HS27 (Mineral fuels). With regard to Angola, 99.3% - 100% of China's total imports from this country were HS27 (Mineral fuels) and for the USA, it was 75.3% - 100%. For total imports from Nigeria, HS27 (Mineral fuels) for most years made up 76.1% - 100% of China's total imports from this country and for the USA, 91.3% - 99.8% for most years. China's total imports from Egypt were mainly made up of HS25[14] in 2001-2007 contributing 35.4% - 69.7% of total imports, after which in 2008-2019, HS27 (Mineral fuels) made up most of the imports with a share of 42.0% - 76.7%. The USA imports from Egypt were dominated by HS62[15] in 2001-2003, after which HS27 (Mineral fuels) were the dominant imports in 2004-2010. In 2011-2018, HS61[16] and HS62 jointly contributed 43.3% - 59.4% of the USA imports from Egypt.

Major imports from South Africa were unique and different from those of the other African countries in that they were more diverse and not

[14] Salt, sulphur, earths and stone, plastering materials, lime & cement.
[15] Articles of apparel & clothing accessories not knitted or crocheted.
[16] Articles of apparel & clothing accessories knitted or crocheted.

dominated by HS27 (Mineral fuels). HS26[17] was China's major import from South Africa, whose import share rose from 35.8% in 2001 to 73.4% by 2019. This was followed by HS72[18], HS74[19], HS51[20], in that order. For the USA, its major imports from South Africa were more diverse and concentrated on non-resource goods, with HS71[21] contributing 20% - 46.1% of the imports; HS87[22] contributing 10.0% - 33.8% of the imports in most years; HS72 accounting for 6.6% - 15.5% of the imports; and HS84[23] with an import share of 5.2% - 10.0% over the years.

As per the product classification by skill and technology intensity (see Table A-6, Appendices), the major imports by both China and the USA from these five African countries, are predominantly Mineral fuels, Non-fuel primary commodities, Resource-intensive manufactures and Low-skill technology intensive manufactured goods. South Africa is the only country from which High-skill, technology-intensive manufactured goods (some of HS84), Medium-skill and technology-intensive goods (some of both HS84 and HS87) form a significant part of imports, and these are imported by the USA. This is expected of imports from South Africa, as it is the African country with a very well developed and diversified industrial base. Therefore, both China and the USA trade with these African countries reinforce these countries as import sources for predominantly minerals and mineral products thereof, as well as low-value added manufactured products. However, when it comes to South Africa, the USA regards South Africa as more than just an import source for basic products, but as a recognisable import source for high value-added manufactures in the form of high-skill and technology-intensive manufactured goods and medium-skill and technology-intensive manufactured goods. Thus, it is the USA-South Africa trade which affords South Africa an opportunity to develop and deepen further its industrial base in order to improve the quality of high value-added

---

[17] Ores, slag and ash.
[18] Iron and steel.
[19] Copper and articles thereof.
[20] Wool, fine or coarse animal hair, horsehair yarn & woven fabric.
[21] Natural or cultured pearls, precious or semi-precious stones, precious metals, metals clad…
[22] Vehicles other than railway or tramway rolling stock, & parts and accessories thereof.
[23] Machinery, mechanical appliances, nuclear reactors, boilers; parts thereof.

manufactured products in the HS84 and HS87 categories to meet import standards for a well-developed and industrialised country like the USA. Therefore, compared to the China-South Africa trade, it is the USA-South Africa trade that is demonstrating more potential in helping South Africa to develop dynamic comparative advantages and thus help the country to deepen its industrial base and achieve its industrial development goals.

4.4.2. Types of Major Exports to Africa by Both China and the USA

Table A-10 (Appendices) shows that most of the products which Africa imports from both the USA and China were high value added manufactured goods classified as High-skill and technology-intensive manufactured goods[24] and the Medium-skill and technology-intensive manufactured goods[25]. This is consistent with the Heckscher-Ohlin theorem because, compared to both China and the USA; Africa is less abundant in modern technology and high-skilled labour, and therefore, would import the goods that uses relatively intensively its relatively scarce factor of production. Over the years, these two categories of high value-added manufactured goods jointly contributed 43.3% - 57.8% of Africa's total imports from the USA and 44.6% - 56.4% of Africa's total imports from China.

Table A-11 (Appendices) shows that with regard to the USA, the top 5 major high value added manufactured imports which Africa obtained from this country were HS84[26], HS87[27], HS85[28], HS88[29] and HS90[30], in that order. The bulk of the imports were from the HS84 product category, which over the years contributed 14.8% - 23.8% of Africa's total imports from the USA. Over the years, these top 5 major product categories, jointly contributed 38.2% - 50.5% of Africa's total imports from the USA. With regard to

---

[24] High skill- and technology-intensive manufactured goods are in product categories HS28-HS39; HS85; HS90; HS91; and very few are in HS84.

[25] Medium skill- and technology-intensive manufactured goods are in product categories HS40; HS84; HS87 and very few are in HS39 and HS85.

[26] HS84 is Machinery, mechanical appliances, nuclear reactors, boilers & parts thereof.

[27] HS87 is Vehicles other than railway or tramway rolling stock, and parts and accessories thereof.

[28] HS85 is Electrical machinery & equipment and parts thereof; sound recorders & reproducers, television.

[29] HS88 is Aircraft, spacecraft, and parts thereof.

[30] HS90 is Optical, photographic, cinematographic, measuring, checking, precision, medical or surgical instruments.

imports from China, the top 5 major high value-added manufactured imports which Africa obtained were HS85, HS84, HS87, HS39 and HS40[31], in that order. The bulk of the imports came from HS85 closely followed by HS84. Jointly, the import share of HS85 and HS84 product categories rose from 26.5% in 2001 to 37.4% by 2019.

Low prices of imported goods, relative to similar and domestically produced goods, benefit African consumers as well as producers who rely on imported inputs and capital goods. Imports of inputs and components for processing and assembly are a major channel for technology transfer in African countries. For many countries, accessing high skill and technologically complex equipment and components through trade has had highly positive economic impacts by facilitating technology transfer and catalysing the development of dynamic comparative advantage.

4.4.3. Intra-Industry Trade Opportunities in the USA-Africa Trade and the China-Africa Trade

When Table A-6 is considered together with Table A-10 (Appendices), the USA-Africa trade in the top 20 products traded, shows that there is both the importing and exporting of high value-added manufactured products from product classification categories HS28, HS29, HS40, HS84, HS85 and HS87. On the other hand, with regard to China-Africa trade in the top 20 products traded, both importing and exporting of high value-added manufactured products is narrower and is limited to product classification categories HS29, HS39 and HS84.

When a country is both exporting and importing products in the same product classification category (goods of similar factor endowment), this is intra-industry trade (IIT). As Appleyard and Field (2017:193) and Mutambara (2013:23) observe, intra-industry trade is more important in manufactured goods than in non-manufactured goods, and especially highest and more important in more sophisticated manufactured goods like Chemicals, Machinery, Transport equipment and Electronics, where economies of scale and product differentiation can be important. In these

[31] HS40 is Rubber and articles thereof.

high value-added and sophisticated manufactured goods, preference diversity and overlapping demand occurs, thus propelling intra-industry trade forward. As Mutambara (2013:32) notes, intra-industry trade unlike inter-industry trade[32] has implications for helping countries to develop deeper and stronger industrial bases. Therefore, where intra-industry trade is a significant part of countries' trade, trade between trading partners becomes more beneficial than where inter-industry trade is the major part of their trade.

Between China and the USA, Tables A-6 and A-10 (Appendices) show that, the USA-Africa trade offers Africa more opportunities for intra-industry trade since both importing and exporting of high value-added manufactured products from similar product classification categories in the top 20 major products is happening over a wider range of high value-added manufactured goods compared to China-Africa trade. Tables A-12, A-13, A-14 and A-15 (Appendices) give some insights into the high value added manufactured goods product categories in which the USA and China have intra-industry trade potentials and opportunities with Africa in general and the African countries in particular.

Very strong intra-industry trade potentials are depicted when the intra-industry trade index (β_i) is equal to or greater than 0.7 (i.e., $0.7 \leq \beta_i \leq 1.0$); moderate levels of intra-industry trade when $0.5 \leq \beta_i \leq 0.69$; and low to very low when $0.1 \leq \beta_i \leq 0.49$). Table A-12 (Appendices) shows that intra-industry trade potentials and opportunities are more prevalent in the USA-Africa trade, than in the China-Africa trade. In the USA-Africa trade, intra-industry trade opportunities and potentials are available in product categories HS28; HS29; HS31; HS33; HS40; HS87 and HS91, where $0.50 \leq (\beta_i) \leq 0.99$ for most years. Such opportunities have been consistently very high in HS29 and HS40 where the IIT indexes are very high; while for most years such opportunities have been moderately high to very high in HS28; HS87; and HS91. After 2010, intra-industry trade potentials in HS31 reduced significantly to range between low to very low, as evidenced by $0.06 \leq (\beta_i) \leq 0.478$. In the China-Africa trade, intra-industry trade opportunities

[32] Inter-industry trade is where a country's exports and imports are in different product classifications, and traditional trade theory deals with this type of trade only.

existed in only one product category, i.e., HS31, and even then, after 2012, such opportunities fell significantly to very low levels as shown by the very low indexes, i.e., $0.012 \leq (\beta_i) \leq 0.209$.

Intra-industry trade opportunities and potentials in the two-way trade in high value-added manufactured goods traded between China and the five major African countries, as well as between the USA and the five major Africa countries are presented in Tables A-13 to A-15 (Appendices). Table A-13 (Appendices) shows that there are very low to no intra-industry trade opportunities in the China-Algeria trade, and while such opportunities were very high in the USA-Algeria trade in HS28 and HS29, such opportunities were sporadic and in very few years, while for most years, there was very low to no intra-industry trade opportunities. Intra-industry trade opportunities in the China-Egypt trade are very high but sporadic in HS28 and HS29 for three and four years, respectively, while for the rest of the years, such opportunities were very low to none. The USA-Egypt trade had moderate to very high intra-industry trade opportunities in HS33. There were very low to no intra-industry trade opportunities in both the China-Angola trade and the USA-Angola trade. Table A-14 (Appendices) show that both the China-Nigeria trade and the USA-Nigeria trade show intra-industry trade opportunities in HS38 and HS34, respectively. The intra-industry trade opportunities in HS38 in the China-Nigeria trade are very high for most years, with $0.7 \leq (\beta_i) \leq 1.0$, while the intra-industry trade opportunities in HS34 in the USA-Nigeria trade are moderate to very high for most years, with $0.558 \leq (\beta_i) \leq 0.922$. However, while intra-industry trade opportunities existed, Nigeria's HS38 exports to China were very low for most years, ranging between US$1 000 and US$37 000.00 per year. Similarly, Nigeria's HS34 exports to the USA were also very low for most years, ranging between US$1 000 and US$200 000.00 per year. Table A-15 (Appendices) shows intra-industry trade opportunities and potentials in both China and the USA trade with South Africa. Moderate to very high intra-industry trade opportunities existed in the China-South Africa trade during the first half of the period considered and this was in HS28; HS29; HS32 and HS38. During the second half of the period considered the levels for intra-industry trade opportunities fell to between low and very low levels, i.e., $0.118 \leq (\beta_i) \leq$

0.497. In the USA-South Africa trade, intra-industry trade opportunities ranged from moderate to very high levels, occurred sporadically during the years, with some opportunities occurring during the earlier years while some opportunities emerged in the later years, and towards the end of the period considered. Such levels of intra-industry trade opportunities were in HS28; HS29; HS32; HS33; HS36; HS38; HS40; HS84 and HS87.

Intra-industry trade allows countries to benefit from large markets of which both China and the USA are. Due to product differentiation, economies of scale, and mutual interdependence on differentiated product varieties, a country can simultaneously produce fewer varieties and produce each variety at a larger scale with increased productivity and lower costs, and thus both expand and deepen their industrial base. As countries depend on each other for differentiated goods, this stimulates innovation as countries specialise within industrial categories. It would also lead to an interchange of knowledge about technology and technological capabilities through joint research as firms in different countries engage in joint research in order to share ideas and better ways of producing high technology and technologically complex products. Intra-industry trade makes transfer of technology much easier, because as Hakura and Jaumotte (1999 cited in Mutambara, 2013a:32), note "a country is more likely to absorb the innovations embodied in foreign technology when it is already engaged in producing and exporting goods from the same product category as those it is importing." Therefore, where intra-industry trade is a significant part of a country's trade, trade with its trading partners becomes more beneficial.

The results presented on intra-industry trade opportunities and potentials in China-Arica trade and USA-Africa trade show that the USA-Africa trade is more likely to expose the Continent to the above benefits that arise from intra-industry trade, and thus help countries to develop deeper and stronger industrial bases. This is because, over the period 2001-2019, the USA-Africa trade presents/or has more opportunities and higher levels of intra-industry trade, as evidenced by the wider range of product categories for which there are higher intra-industry trade indexes. The results also show that, among the five major African countries with which China and the USA trade, the USA-South Africa has more potential for intra-industry trade, and thus has the potential and opportunities to help South Africa to harness more fully the benefits that arise from intra-industry trade and thus help to deepen its industrial base.

Implications of intra-industry trade on industrial development is correlated with trade intensity. Therefore, as Koçyiğit and Sen (2007 cited in Mutambara, 2013a:24) note, "As the volume of trade with trading partners increases, there will be more opportunities for more differentiated goods to be traded", thus enabling the trading countries to utilise more the benefits which arise from intra-industry trade. Table A-16 (Appendices) shows that, compared to China, the USA's trade with Africa promotes an increasing share of high value-added manufactured exports to the USA, with such a share rising from 5.84% of Africa's total exports to the USA in 2001 to 15.01% by 2019. The same can be said of the USA-South Africa trade with the share of high value-added manufactured exports to the USA ranged between 24.77% and 51.81% in the period 2001-2019. On the other hand, with China there has been a continuous fall in the share of high value-added manufactured exports from South Africa to China, falling from 20.94% in 2001 to 2.90% by 2019. Therefore, given the observation about the volume of trade and opportunities for more differentiated goods traded, the USA-Africa trade and the USA-South Africa trade have the potential and opportunities to help Africa in general and South Africa in particular to harness more the intra-industry trade benefits needed to promote and facilitate industrial development in those product categories in which such intra-industry trade opportunities and potentials exist. As the share of high value-added manufactured exports that enter the USA market continues to rise, so would the motivation to simultaneously produce fewer varieties and produce each variety at a larger scale with increased productivity so as to improve competitiveness on entering the USA market.

While the USA-Africa trade and the USA-South Africa trade show that there are a lot more intra-industry trade opportunities and potentials, intra-industry trade is yet to be a significant component of Africa's (and South Africa's) trade with the USA. Currently, a significant part of USA-Africa trade, as well as USA trade with the five major African countries it trades with, is still mainly inter-industry trade, just as is China-Africa trade and

China's trade with the five major African countries. As shown in Section 4.4.1, inter-industry trade confines Africa into a source for raw materials, resource-intensive manufactured goods and low value added manufactured goods; and continuing to specialise in such products does not necessarily help to deepen and to develop further the level of industrial development.

4.5. Trade Intensity

Examining trade introversion between the USA and the African countries and between China and the African countries helps to illustrate the status of trade linkages between these trading partners, and thus give some insights into the extent to which trade between them is biased towards each other. Furthermore, trade introversion between both China and the USA with Africa is also examined to gain insights into the extent to which trade by either is biased towards the African Continent compared to the rest of the world. Trade intensity is a two-way measurement, e.g., region i's trade intensity towards region j, and region j' trade intensity toward region i. Since the revealed trade preference (RTP) index is used, $RTP_{ij} = RTP_{ji}$ independently of the region's size, it is not necessary to compute the relative bilateral trade intensity from the perspective of both regions[33].

4.5.1. Trade Intensity with Major Trading Countries in Africa

Table A-17 (Appendices) shows the revealed trade preference index (RTP_{ij}) results for China and the five countries. Trade orientation has been highest with Angola, followed by South Africa. In China-Angola trade, $0.85 \leq RTP_{ij} \leq 1.00$. Trade orientation has been highest with Angola because China and Angola are intertwined through crude oil because this is, and has been, the single most significant commodity that has been a key factor in the expansion of the Sino-Angolan economic relationship, and China has remained a significant player in Angola's economy. The resource-for-infrastructure deals have enabled Angola to pay for infrastructure that China

[33] However, where this is done, the results confirm that $RTP_{ij} = RTP_{ji}$ independently of the region's size.

built in Angola through supplying China with resources. China's loan-for-oil deals with Angola promote the flow of crude oil from Angola into China since China's loans are an attractive alternative to those from international institutions that can have democratic-promoting strings attached.

With China-South Africa trade, $0.29 \leq RTP_{ij} \leq 0.76$, with trade orientation towards South Africa rising over the years. Trade orientation towards South Africa rose significantly after 2010 when China became South Africa's number one trading partner, with the index rising to $0.62 \leq RTP_{ij} \leq 0.76$. South Africa's acceptance into BRICS in December 2010 has also helped in deepening trade relations with China. Of the five African countries China trades mostly with, China's trade is least oriented towards Algeria with results of $-0.36 \leq RTP_{ij} \leq 0.31$. A common phenomenon in China's trade orientation with these five African countries is that, especially after 2011, China's trade orientation to these countries improved, especially with Algeria with whom trade orientation had been negative, and with Nigeria with whom trade orientation had been very low. Improved and rising trade orientation towards each of these countries is consistent with (and thus mirrors) the results presented in Sections 4.3.1 – 4.3.6 with regard to the rise in the value of China's trade with each of these countries over the years, as shown by the continuous rise in China's trade shares in the African countries total trade.

Table A-18 (Appendices) shows the revealed trade preference index (RTP_{ij}) results for the USA and the five African countries. The results show that the USA's trade orientation with these five countries has been highest with Nigeria followed closely by with Angola. Trade orientation was highest with Nigeria in 2001-2011, with $0.73 \leq RTP_{ij} \leq 0.93$. After 2011, the USA trade orientation towards Nigeria has been falling continuously, until $RTP_{ji} = 0.18$ in 2019. USA trade orientation was highest with Angola in 2001-2011, with $0.69 \leq RTP_{ij} \leq 1.00$, after which USA trade orientation towards Angola fell continuously, until $RTP_{ji} = -0.07$ in 2018. Of the five countries, the results show that over the years, in general, USA trade orientation has been least towards South Africa, with $0.14 \leq RTP_{ij} \leq 0.36$, with such trade orientation deteriorating after 2008 to $RTP_{ij} = 0.14$ in 2019. A common phenomenon in the USA's trade orientation with these five African countries is that, after 2011, USA trade orientation towards each of these countries has been on a continuous decline. This is consistent with (and thus mirrors) the results presented in Sections 4.3.1 – 4.3.6 which show that from 2011 onwards, there was a continuous decline in the USA trade shares in the African countries total trade.

These results show that for China, Angola and South Africa have over the years, remained as significant trading partners with China. Through improved trade engagements with Algeria, Egypt and Nigeria, the importance of these countries as trade partners with China has been improving, as evidenced by the rising revealed trade preference indexes. However, the opposite has been happening with the USA. USA trade was well oriented towards the five major African countries during the first half of the 21st century, showing that these countries and the USA regarded each other as significant trading partners, and especially with Angola and Nigeria. However, unlike China who maintained its significant trade relations with Angola and South Africa and in the process engaged more with the other countries and thus earned them as significant trading partners, the USA disengaged in its trade orientation towards all these five countries during the second half of the 21st century. As such, all the five African countries and the USA have become less relevant as trading partners to each other.

4.5.2. Trade Intensity with Africa

Tables A-19 and A-20 (Appendices) show the results of China and USA trade introversion with regard to the African Continent. The results show that the status of China-Africa trade linkages and that of USA-Africa trade linkages are very different. The RTP_{ij} results of USA-Africa trade and China-Africa trade show that China's trade is more oriented towards Africa than the USA's trade is to Africa. Table A-19 (Appendices) shows that trade intensity in the China-Africa trade has been on a consistent rise, rising from $RTP_{ij} = 0.36$ in 2001 to $RTP_{ij} = 0.62$ in 2019. Therefore, China and Africa regard each other as significant trading partners as their trade is significantly oriented towards each other as shown by the RTP_{ij} results. These results which depict increased orientation of China's trade to Africa are consistent with (and mirror) the results presented in Section 4.1 which show that, over the years, the share of China-Africa trade in Africa's total trade has been on a continuous rise.

After Africa, China's trade is also oriented towards America[34], with $0.31 \leq RTP_{ij} \leq 0.47$, as well as towards the Organisation of the Petroleum Exporting Countries[35] (OPEC) with $0.22 \leq RTP_{ij} \leq 0.53$, where for the latter it is due to China's ever-increasing energy needs. China's trade is not oriented towards Europe, with $-0.25 \leq RTP_{ij} \leq -0.10$. Compared with these other three regions, China's trade is most oriented towards Africa. Therefore, the China-Africa trade is more beneficial to China, as according to trade theory, a trading partner tends to benefit more from trade with those partners it trades more intensively as trade resistances are lower. Africa is a resource-rich continent, which China relies on to satisfy some of its strong demand for resources and raw materials, and as Section 4.4.1 above shows, China's major imports from Africa are more concentrated in the primary sector.

For the USA and Africa, Table A-20 (Appendices) shows the RTP_{ij} results, and these show that trade intensity between the USA and Africa has been on a constant decline. The beginning of the USA-Africa trade disengagement occurred in 2012 with the index drastically falling from $RTP_{ij} = 0.42$ in 2001 to $RTP_{ij} = 0.24$ in 2012, after which it continued to fall rapidly with each year down to $RTP_{ij} = -0.03$ by 2019. Therefore, after 2012, the USA-Africa trade has not been oriented towards each other and as such, the two regions have not been significant trading partners. The decline in the USA trade orientation with Africa is consistent with (and mirrors) the results in Section 4.1 which show that over the years, the share of USA-Africa trade in Africa's total trade has been on a continuous decline, with a significant decline experienced from 2012 onwards, just as also reflected in the RTP_{ij} indexes.

Compared to Africa, USA trade is more oriented towards Asia, with $0.35 \leq RTP_{ij} \leq 0.57$. Unlike with Africa, the USA's trade has, over the years,

[34] This includes all the 47 countries, i.e., the USA, Canada, South American countries, as well as other territories and Islands that make up America.

[35] Currently the organisation comprises 15 member countries, i.e., Algeria, Angola, Republic of Congo (i.e., Congo, Brazzaville), Ecuador, Equatorial Guinea, Gabon, Islamic Republic of Iran, Iraq, Kuwait, Libya, Nigeria, Qatar, Saudi Arabia, United Arab Emirates and Venezuela.

become more and more oriented towards Europe, with the RTP_{ij} index rising from RTP_{ij} = 0.17 in 2001 to RTP_{ij} = 0.31 by 2019. However, like with Africa, the USA trade orientation with OPEC has been on a continuous decline over the years, with the RTP_{ij} index falling continuously from RTP_{ij} = 0.61 in 2001 to RTP_{ij} = 0.01 by 2019. Therefore, with regard to these four regions, the USA trade is mostly oriented towards Asia followed by Europe, and least with Africa.

China and Africa's trade is more oriented towards each other because as Mutambara (2013b:274-275) notes, several African countries have adopted the "Look East" policy where African countries seek to engage more with Asia than their traditional "Northern" trading partners. Pursuing the "Look East" policy serves to reinforce even further the orientation of China and Africa trade towards each other. In addition, the Forum on China Africa Cooperation (FOCAC) has been a key instrument in facilitating China-Africa trade and other economic relations, thus contributing to China's increasing trade orientation towards Africa, as it has been noted that after FOCAC was launched in 2000, bilateral trade between China and Africa increased significantly. The bilateral trade agreements which China has with the African countries, China's Duty-Free Quota-Free (DFQF) programme, as well as, the other trade facilitating measures China has put in place to give further support to increase and expand Africa's exports into China, have also helped to improve China and Africa trade orientation towards each other.

The strategic interaction and linking of trade, FDI and financial aid in China's Africa policy contributes to and facilitates the high levels of China-Africa trade orientation. As Busse, et al (2014:8), Pigato and Tang (2015:10) and other authors have noted, the traditional focus of Chinese government-led FDI in Africa has been on natural resources[36] and related infrastructure[37] necessary for the extraction and transportation of oil, minerals, and other natural resources. Thus, the bulk of Chinese investment focuses on a few resource-rich countries of which South Africa is the top destination, with both Nigeria and Angola also receiving significant amounts. Furthermore,

[36] Pigato and Tang (2015:10) note that 30% of Chinese investment in Africa is in extractive industries.

[37] Chinese companies building pipelines, power stations, roads, railways and seaports.

Busse, et al. (2014:7, 8) and Pigato and Tang (2015:16) note that Chinese companies often work on contracted projects as a result of a greater finance or trade deal the Chinese government agreed upon with the government of a particular African country which entail some sort of economic or technical cooperation. Lines of credit, often at concessional rates, are given to the government of a resource-rich country and these credit lines are secured by long-term agreements on resource rights. Therefore, as often observed, some Chinese state-owned firms build large-scale infrastructure in African countries in exchange for access to minerals or hydrocarbons, such as oil and other resources. Thus, the resource-rich countries in Africa use those minerals, hydrocarbons and other resources directly as a way to pay for the infrastructure built by Chinese firms[38]. Therefore, one can argue that these resource-for-infrastructure contracts (or resource-for-infrastructure deals)[39] and the tight and strategic link between credit lines and resources contribute to China's trade orientation towards Africa.

The "The China-Africa Swap" which is to replace (and is already replacing) the resource-for-infrastructure deals, also has implications for increasing China's and Africa's trade orientation towards each other, because it too facilitates exports from Africa into China, as supply of resources is used to settle loans given in advance. Olander (2020a; 2020b) notes that for the past two or three years, China has been working on a new financing model to replace the resource-for-infrastructure deals, called the "The China-Africa Swap." The swap formula provides loans in advance for African countries' development projects at a completely fixed price for the settled supply of resources. African governments can invest in public works now, and pay for them with future exports. The swap formula allows African

[38] Some of the examples are soft loans to Angola repaid in oil at fixed prices (Busse, et al., 2014:8); the Congo River dam in the Republic of Congo being financed by the China Exim Bank loans backed by guarantees of crude oil, Bui Dam in Ghana also being financed by China Exim Bank backed by guarantees of cocoa, and the loan for Souapiti Dam in Guinea which is linked to mining revenue from Bauxite (IDE-JETRO, 2009:70).

[39] Also known as the "Angola Model." In mid-2000s, the Chinese identified Angola as a potentially major supplier of oil. Since Angola needed to rebuild its infrastructure after decades of civil war that ended in 2002, China offered to rebuild Angola's infrastructure, set a price for all infrastructure to be provided and then Angola would pay with oil rather than cash (Olander, 2020a).

leaders to leverage their resource wealth as collateral to access credit at a manageable interest rate as well as a viable reimbursement option. For China, the formula offers a solution to vital resources; and for African nations, a solution for a loan-free means and an avenue to transform the continent's natural resources advantage into development advantage by using the loans to build productive infrastructure and other projects.

The USA has trade facilitating and promotion measures in place to enhance USA-Africa trade. As noted in Section 2.1.2; only five African countries are not beneficiaries of the Generalised Systems of Preferences (GSP), the largest and oldest USA preferential trade treatment program to help beneficiary countries to increase and diversify their trade with the United States. To augment the GSPs in facilitating USA-Africa trade, the African Growth and Opportunity Act (AGOA) signed in May 2000 and now extended to 2025 has become the most notable United States' instrument centred at facilitating trade engagements with Africa and 38 African countries are currently eligible for this programme. The Trade and Investment Framework Agreements (TIFAs) are also there to facilitate trade between the USA and individual countries, as well as with regional economic integration arrangements in Africa. While all these initiatives helped USA and Africa's trade to be oriented towards each other in 2001-2011, after 2011, these same initiatives have not been able to sustain the USA-Africa trade orientation momentum towards each other, as evidenced by drastic and the continuous decline in the RTP_{ij} index for USA-Africa trade since after 2011.

4.6. Ease of Market Access

Revealed Trade Barrier (RTB) indexes were calculated and used to determine the existence of trade barriers between the blocs as well as to gain insights into the extent of ease of market access by Africa's products into both the Chinese and USA markets. This is important to consider because eliminating tariff and non-tariff barriers by both the USA and China helps to increase their trade with Africa. For African countries, this would create a bigger market for their products, since as individuals; the USA and China are huge markets that African countries can benefit from accessing more easily. Furthermore, examining the RTB indexes over the period 2001-2019, helps to determine whether, over the years, China and the USA have been allowing more access into their respective markets to the products originating from the African countries. The reduction and eventual removal of trade barriers has implications for greater welfare effects.

As already noted in Section 4.4.1, Mineral fuels, Non-fuel primary commodities, and Resource–intensive manufactured goods dominate both the USA and China's top 20 major imports from Africa. The results from the revealed trade barriers (RTB^{j}_{ik}) indexes, as presented in Tables A-21 and A-22 (Appendices) show that most of these raw materials and low value-added imports by the USA and China experience preferential treatment when entering both the USA and Chinese markets. For those imported by China, Table A-21 (Appendices) shows evidence as given by $RTB^{j}_{ik} > 1$ for HS27, HS26, HS74, HS81, HS44, HS52 and HS51 throughout the period 2001-2019. For most years, $RTB^{j}_{ik} > 1$ for HS12, HS27, HS75 and HS41. Therefore, 11 out of 17 of the product categories for raw materials and low value-added imports by China experience preferential treatment when entering the Chinese market. For those imported by the USA, Table A-22 (Appendices) shows evidence of preferential access where $RTB^{j}_{ik} > 1$ for HS27, HS71 and HS18 throughout the period 2001-2019. For most years, $RTB^{j}_{ik} > 1$ for HS62, HS26, HS61, HS09, HS25 and HS57. Therefore, 9 out of 15 of the product categories for raw materials and low-value added imports by the USA experience preferential treatment when entering the USA market. For both China and the USA, those products prone to Sanitary and Phytosanitary (SPS) measures[40] are not given preferential treatment, as evidenced by $RTB^{j}_{ik} < 1$ for HS03, HS08, HS15, and HS40.

Section 4.1.4 above shows that a few High-skill technology-intensive manufactured goods, and Medium-skill technology-intensive manufactured

---

[40] SPS measures are quarantine and biosecurity measures which are applied to protect human, animal or plant life or health from risks arising from the introduction, establishment and spread of pests and diseases and from risks arising from additives, toxins and contaminants in food and feed.

goods, in the form of Transport and equipment, Chemicals and Polymers, Machinery, Electrics and Electronics, form a small part of both the USA and China top 20 imports from Africa. The results from the RTB^j_{ik} indexes for these high value-added manufactured goods show that these products are mainly discriminated against upon entry into both the USA and Chinese markets. However, the indexes show that the level of discrimination is experienced a lot more when entering the Chinese market than the USA market. For example, Table A-21 (Appendices) shows that the high value-added manufactured goods imported by China are HS29, HS39 and HS84, and each of them is highly discriminated against, as shown by $0.02 \leq RTB^j_{ik} \leq 0.24$ for HS29; $0.03 \leq RTB^j_{ik} \leq 0.15$ for HS39; and $0.01 \leq RTB^j_{ik} \leq 0.11$ for HS84. Table A-22 (Appendices) shows that the high value-added manufactured goods imported by the USA are HS28, HS29, HS84, HS85 and HS87. While each of these are discriminated against upon entry into the USA market, the level of discrimination is much lower compared to that by China. For example, $0.36 \leq RTB^j_{ik} \leq 1.87$ for HS28, with products from this category experiencing preferential treatment when accessing the USA market in 2001, 2002, 2014, 2015, 2018 and 2019 as evidenced by $RTB^j_{ik} > 1$ in these years. For HS29, the level of discrimination is reflected by $0.17 \leq RTB^j_{ik} \leq 0.77$, with the level of discrimination reduced in the period 2014-2019. HS84 and HS85 are greatly discriminated against, to almost the same level as by China, with $0.04 \leq RTB^j_{ik} \leq 0.33$ for HS84, and $0.01 \leq RTB^j_{ik} \leq 0.08$ for HS85. HS87 is also discriminated against with $0.07 \leq RTB^j_{ik} \leq 0.76$.

Therefore, the relatively lower levels of discrimination by the USA on some of these product categories compared to China, show that it is the USA which provides Africa with more room and easier market access for the Continent's high MVA products, thus giving Africa an incentive to continue to modernise and improve the technological complexity of its manufactured products. This is important for Africa so that the Continent does not continue to remain largely as an import source for raw materials and low value added manufactured goods. The importance of the USA in providing a market for manufactured goods from Africa is also noted by Mutambara (2013b:291, 293) where Europe and the USA were seen to be significant markets for Africa's total export earnings from manufactured products. Improving the level of industrial development and the technology complexity of Africa's manufacturing sector is important, as intra-industry trade would become a significant component of Africa's trade with both the USA and China. As pointed out in Section 4.4.3, intra-industry trade promotes innovation and an interchange of knowledge and technology, all of which is essential for improvements in industry performance.

4.7. Trade Complementarity

Trade complementarity indexes (TCI) show how well the structure of country j exports match (or complement) the import requirements of country i. Thus, the TCI approximate the adequacy of country j's export supply to country i's import demand by calculating the extent to which country i's total imports match country j's total exports. The results in Table A-23 (Appendices) approximate the adequacy of China's export supply to Africa's import demand, as well as the adequacy of the USA's export supply to Africa's import demand. For both China and the USA, the TCI are calculated from Africa's perspective in order to show or indicate trade complementarity from Africa's perspective. By computing TCI over a period, it can be determined whether trade between China and Africa and between the USA and Africa has become more or less complementary over time.

Tables A-23 and A-24 (Appendices) show that both China and USA export supply matches very well Africa's import demand in all product categories. This is evidenced by very high trade complementarity indexes in all product categories. Table A-23 (Appendices) shows that across product categories, with regards to China, $81.02\% \leq TCI \leq 99.98\%$; while Table A-24 (Appendices) show that with the USA, $94.17\% \leq TCI \leq 99.99\%$, across product categories. Thus, the high trade complementarity indexes show that there are opportunities for Africa to increase its trade with both China and the USA since the export supply of these countries match Africa's import demand very well. Furthermore, trade theory argues that, where trade complementarity exists there are high opportunities for trade, but an absence of trade complementarity would lead to low opportunities for trade.

In addition, results from trade complementarity indexes are useful to suggest where further development of trade relations would be economically beneficial for both countries; and the very high TCI results across product categories in Tables A-23 and A-24 (Appendices) show that trade relations could be developed further in all product categories. Table A-25 (Appendices) shows that it is in the China-Africa trade that trade has been developed further in some of the product categories. This is evidenced by the significant increase in the import share of some of the products imported from China in Africa' total world imports of those products. For example; (i) for Textile fibres, yarn, fabrics and clothing (SITC 26 + 65 + 84), the share of Africa's imports from China in Africa's world imports of this product category rose from 10.62% in 2001 to 44.75% in 2019; (ii) the import share for Iron and steel (SITC 67) rose from 1.45% in 2001 to 26.30% in 2019; (iii) the import share of Other manufactured goods (SITC 6 + 8 less 667 and 68) rose from 7.92% in 2001 to 33.19% in 2019; and (iv) for Machinery and transport equipment (SITC 7), the import share rose from 3.64% in 2001 to 25.08% in 2019. Moderate increases were experienced in Non-ferrous metals (SITC 68) where the import share rose from 3.38% in 2001 to 16.30% in 2019; and in Chemicals (SITC 5) where the import share rose from 2.69% in 2001 to 12.11% in 2019. On the other hand, while the USA export supply matches Africa's import demand very well in all product categories as indicated by the high trade complementarity indexes across all product categories, Table A-26 (Appendices) show that there has not been any further development of trade in any of these product categories. This is evidenced by the generally low import shares in most product categories and have not shown any significant change over the years. Furthermore, there has been a significant fall in the import shares of some of the products imported from the USA in Africa's total world imports of those products.

For example: Food, basic (SITC 0 + 22 + 4) whose import share fell from 12.36% in 2001 to 5.77% in 2019, and Machinery and transport equipment (SITC 7) whose import share fell from 13.45% in 2001 to 7.04% in 2019.

By matching very well the import demand for Africa and thus meeting some of that import demand in order to augment supplies provided by domestic producers in the Africa countries, these imports contribute toward lower producer price inflation in Africa, which in turn contributes to a moderation in consumer price increases. The relatively lower prices for imported goods benefit African consumers, as well as producers who rely on imported inputs and capital goods. Where the imports are inputs and components for processing and assembly, these become a major channel for technology transfer in many countries. For example imports of: (i) Parts and components for electrical and electronic goods (SITC 759 + 764 + 772 + 776)[41]; (ii) Other medium-skill and high-skill technology-intensive industrial machinery and parts, which are part of the imports in Machinery and transport equipment (SITC 7) category; and (ii) Organic and inorganic chemicals, as well as Medicinal and pharmaceutical products, which are part of the imports in Chemical products (SITC 5) category. Machinery and transport equipment (SITC 7) imports of (i) Electronic, excluding parts and components (SITC 751 + 752 + 761 + 762 + 763 + 775)[42], and (ii) both Medium-skill and High-skill technology-intensive imports of Power generating machinery and equipment, Specialised machinery, Metal working machinery, Electrical machinery, apparatus and appliances, n.e.s; have highly positive economic impacts by facilitating technology transfer and catalysing the development of dynamic comparative advantage. Other imports in Machinery and transport equipment (SITC 7) like Office machines and automatic data processing machines and Telecommunication and sound recording apparatus, help to improve operational and production efficiency in the various organisations.

---

[41] SITC (772) are Medium-skill and technology-intensive, while (SITC 759 + 764 + 776) are High-skill and technology-intensive.

[42] SITC 775 are Medium-skill and technology-intensive, while SITC 751 + 752 + 761 + 762 + 763) are High-skill and technology-intensive.

CONCLUSION

Both the USA and China have in place trade facilitating instruments that they use to promote their respective trade with African countries. To facilitate and promote trade with Africa, China uses trade initiatives like the Forum on China-Africa Cooperation, bilateral trade agreements entered into with various African countries, China's Duty-Free Quota-Free (DFQF) Programme, as well as other trade facilitating measures like holding African commodity exhibitions, establishing African product exhibition centres and offering free stalls or reducing stall rents. With such trade facilitating instruments in place, China's trade is oriented towards Africa as evidenced by the high RTP_{ij} indexes. As China has continued to engage more vigorously with African countries over the years, its trade has become even more oriented towards Africa, as evidenced by the continuous rise in the RTP_{ij} indexes. The USA promotes trade with Africa through the Africa Growth and Opportunity Act program; the Generalised System of Preferences program; Trade and Investment Framework Agreements. While these initiatives helped to grow USA-Africa trade over the years, resulting in rising USA trade orientation towards Africa, this only occurred up 2011, after which USA trade ceased to be oriented towards Africa, as evidenced by continuous decline in RTP_{ij} indexes.

The trade complementarity indexes show that Africa's import demand is matched very well by both China's export supply and the USA's export supply, therefore showing that it is possible for both China-Africa trade and USA-Africa trade to be increased and developed further. Matching Africa's import demand helps to augment domestic supply, thus reduce producer price inflation, and thus benefit both producers and consumers. Where the imports are inputs and components for processing and assembly, as well as medium-skill and high-skill technology-intensive industrial machinery and equipment, this would facilitate technology transfer and catalysing the development of dynamic comparative advantages. Because Africa and China's trade are more oriented towards each other, it is with China that Africa is utilising the complementarity between its import demand and China's export supply to develop further its trade with China. This is shown by Africa increasing the percentage shares of some of those imports that complement its import demand from China and not the USA.

For both the USA and China, their major imports from Africa are natural resource based especial Mineral fuels (HS27) as well as a resource-intensive goods and low value-added manufactured goods; while Africa mainly imports medium-skill and high-skill technology-intensive manufactured goods from China and the USA. Thus, due to the vast differences in the levels of industrial development between China and Africa and between the USA and Africa, both China-Africa trade and USA-Africa trade are mainly inter-industry. However, the results from the intra-industry trade indexes show that there are opportunities for intra-industry trade, although these opportunities are very few. Such opportunities are in USA-Africa trade as well as in the USA-South Africa trade. Intra-industry trade is beneficial for transfer of technology, sharing of knowledge and skills as well as to facilitate joint research in science and technology, all of which is essential to modernise and develop further a country's industrial base. Therefore, it is USA's trade with Africa which is more relevant in helping Africa to utilise and realise more fully the industrial development benefits that arise from utilising intra-industry trade opportunities. This is important for Africa so that it can create and utilise dynamic comparative advantages and thus cease to serve mainly as an import source for unprocessed natural resources, resource-intensive goods and low value-added manufactured goods.

The results from the revealed trade barriers indexes show that most raw materials, resource-intensive goods and low-value added goods imported by the USA and China experience preferential treatment when entering both markets. The USA and China are huge markets that Africa benefits from accessing more easily. High value-added manufactured goods are mainly discriminated against upon entry into either the USA or China. However, the level of discrimination is experienced a lot more when entering the Chinese market than the USA market. Therefore, it is the USA that provides Africa with more room and easier market access for high MVA products, thus giving Africa an incentive to continue to modernise and improve the technological complexity of its manufactured products. This is important for

Africa so that it does not continue to remain largely as an import source for raw materials and low value-added manufactured goods.

References

Alden, Chris and Yu-Shan Wu. 2014. "South Africa and China: the making of a partnership." *South African Institute of International Affairs (SAIIA) Occasional paper no.199*. Global Powers and Africa Programme.

American Chamber of Commerce in Egypt. 2020. *Egypt-US trade & investment relations profile.* Available: https://www.amcham.org.eg/information-resources/trade-resources/egypt-us-relations/trade-investment-relations-profile#egypt-us-investment Accessed on March 16, 2021.

Ajayi, Olalekan A. 2020. *Inducement beyond China-Africa economic partnership: a case study of China-Nigeria relations*. Bachelor thesis. Kaunas: Department of Regional Studies, Vytautas Magnus University.

Agbebi, Motolani and Petri Virtanen. 2017. "Dependency Theory – A Conceptual Lens to Understand China's Presence in Africa?" *Forum for Development Studies*. 44(3): 429-451.

Appleyard, Dennis R., and Field, Alfred J. 2017. *International Economics*, (9e). McGraw-Hill Irwin, USA.

Badri, Mohamed E. 2020. "Egypt and China: Historical relationship into the future." *Global Times*. Available at: https://www.globaltimes.cn/content/1189854.shtml. Accessed on: March 16, 2021.

Bano, Sayeed. 2014. "An empirical examination of trade relations between New Zealand and China in the context of a Free Trade Area," *Working Paper in Economics,* 04/14. Department of Economics, University of Waikato, New Zealand.

Broadbent, Meredith. 2011. "The role of FTA negotiations in the future of US-Egypt relations." *A report of the CSIS Scholl Chair in International business*. Centre for Strategic and International Studies (CSIS).

Burke, Christopher, Sanusha Naidu, and Arno Nepgen, A. 2008. "Scoping study on China's relations with South Africa." *AERC Scoping Studies on China-Africa Economic Relations*. African Economic Research Consortium (AERC), Nairobi.

Busse, Matthias, Ceren Erdogan, and Henning Mühlen. 2014. "China's impact on Africa – The role of trade, FDI and Aid." *IEE Working Paper*. Volume | 206, BOCHUM 2014.

Calabrese, John. 2021. *The new Algeria and China*. Available at: https://www.mei.edu/publications/new-algeria-and-china. Accessed on March 22, 2021.

Campbell, Horace. 2008. "China in Africa: challenging US global hegemony." *Third World Quarterly*. 29(1): 89-105. Accessed on December 25, 2020. https://doi.org/10.1080/01436590701726517.

Chingarande, Anna., Macleans Mzumara, and Roseline Karambakuwa. 2013. "Comparative advantage and economic performance of East African Community (EAC) member states." *Journal of Economics*. 4(1): 39-46.

Cook, Nicolas. 2020. "South Africa: current issues, economy and U.S. relations." *Congressional Research Service. R45687*. Available at: https://fas.org/sgp/crs/row/R45687.pdf Accessed on November 3, 2020.

Cooke, Jennifer G. 2013. "US engagement in Africa." *Politique étrangère*. 2013/2 Summer Issue (2):67-79. [*Foreign politics*]

Corkin, Lucy. 2008. "AERC scoping exercise on China-Africa relations: The case of Angola." *AERC Scoping Studies on China-Africa Economic Relations*, African Economic Research Consortium (AERC), Nairobi.

Dahshan, Mohamed E. 2021. *Egyptian Exceptionalism in a Chinese-led World*. Available at: https://www.chathamhouse.org/2021/02/egyptian-exceptionalism-chinese-led-world?gclid=EAIaIQobChMIq MqrquK07wIVCLTtCh1HAAnwEAAYASAAEgJSe_D_BwE Accessed on March 16, 2021.

Eisenman, Joshua. 2012. "China-Africa trade patterns: causes and consequences." *Journal of Contemporary China* (2012), 21(77), September, 793–810.

Ferreira, Manuel E. 2008. "China in Angola: Just a passion for oil?" *China returns to Africa: A rising power and a Continent embrace,* edited by Chris Alden, Daniel Large, and Ricardo Soares de Oliveira, pages 295-317.

Gadallah, Yasser M. 2016. "An analysis of the evolution of Sino-Egyptian economic relations." In *Toward Well-Oiled Relations: China's Presence in the Middle East Following the Arab Spring,* edited by Niv Horesh, Pages 94-114. The Nottingham China Policy Institute Series. Palgrave Macmillan in the UK.

Grubel, Hebert G., and Peter J Lloyd. 1975. *Intra-industry trade: The theory and measurement of international trade in differentiated products.* McMillan, London.

Hamanaka, Shintaro. 2015. "The selection of trade integration indicators: Intraregional share, Intensity, Homogeneous intensity, and Introversion Index." *ADB Economics Working Paper Series, No. 455.* [Online]. Available: http://hdl.handle.net/10419/128569. Accessed January 20, 2020.

Hamaizia, Adel. 2020. *Rebalancing Algeria's economic relations with China.* Available at: https://www.chathamhouse.org/2020/12/rebalancing-algerias-economic-relations-china Accessed on March 22, 2021.

Hatab, Assem A. 2012. "Exploring Egypt-China bilateral trade: dynamics and prospect." *Journal of Economic Studies.* 39(3): 314 – 326.

Hu, Weining, 2017. *New import measures in China to benefit African, Southeast Asian exporters.* Available: http://China-briefing.com/new-import-measures-in-china-to-benefit-african-southeast-asian-exporters/. Accessed on January 14, 2021.

Iapadre, Lelio P., and Lucia Tajoli. 2013. “Emerging countries and trade liberalisation: A network analysis.” *Journal of Policy Modelling*. 36S (2014) S89-S110.

Iapadre, Lelio., and Francesca Tironi. 2009. Measuring trade regionalism: The case of Asia. *UNU-CRIS Working Papers. W-2009/9*. United Nations University – Comparative Regional Integration Studies, BE – Belgium.

Iapadre, Lelio. 2006. “Regional integration agreements and the geography of world trade: Statistical indicators and empirical evidence.” In *Assessment and Measurement of Regional Integration,* edited by Philippe De Lombaerde, Pages. 67-85. Routledge, OXON OX14 4RN.

Iapadre, Lelio. 2004. Regional integration arrangements and the geography of world trade: Measurement problems and empirical evidence. *UNU-CRIS e-Working Papers. W-2004/3*. United Nations University.

Ibrahim, Kabiru H., and Abdulaziz Shebu. 2016. “Nigeria-India bilateral trade relations: an analysis of trade complementarity index (TCI).” *Asian Journal of Economic Modelling*. 4(4): 190-198.

Institute of Developing Economies-Japan External Trade Organisation (IDE-JETRO). 2009. *China in Africa: A Strategic Overview* (September 2009). Available at: https://www.ide.go.jp/library/English/Data/Africa_file/Manualreport/pdf/china_all.pdf or https://www.ide.go.jp/English/Data/Africa_file/Manualreport/cia.html. Accessed on April 23, 2021.

Jones, Vivian C., and Brock R. Williams. 2012. U.S. Trade and Investment Relations with sub-Saharan Africa and the African Growth and Opportunity Act. *Congressional Report Service Report for Congress*. 7-5700 RL31772.

Kalaba, Mmatlou., Ron Sandrey, and Dirk Ernst van Seventer. 2005. *Analysis of trade between South Africa and the EU and a preliminary attempt to examine the impact of the EU-SA FTA. Trade and Industrial Policy Strategies*. Available at: http://www.tips.org.za/research-archive/trade-and-industry/item/738-analysis-of-trade-between-south-africa-and-the-eu-and-a-preliminary-attempt-to-examine-the-impact-of-the-eu-sa-fta-on-trade. Accessed on December 10, 2019.

Leamer, Edward E. 1995. "The Heckscher-Ohlin model in theory and practice." *Princeton Studies in International Finance* No. 77.

Loertscher, Rudolf and Frank Wolter. 1980. "Determinants of Intra-Industry Trade: Among Countries and across Industries", *Weltwirtschaftliches Archiv*, 1980, Bd. 116, H. 2 (1980), pp. 280-293. URL: https://www.jstor.org/stable/40438460. [*World Economic Archive*]

Mba, Ike N. 2013. "US economic policy towards Nigeria: implications, pros & cons." *Journal of Law, Policy and Globalisation.* Vol.16, 2013: 30-34. Available at: https://core.ac.uk/download/pdf/234649682.pdf. Accessed on November 3, 2020.

Mabrouk, Mirette F. 2019. *Trade, Reform, and Revitalization: Toward a US-Egypt Free Trade Agreement.* Available at: https://mei.edu/publications/us-egypt-fta Accessed on March 16, 2021.

Malaquais Assis. 2011. *Angola's foreign policy: Pragmatic recalibrations. South African Institute of International Affairs (SAIIA) Occasional paper no.84.* South African Foreign Policy Drivers Programme. Available at: https://media.africaportal.org/documents/saia_sop_84_malaquias_20110531.pdf. Accessed on November 23, 2020.

Mikic, Mia and John Gilbert. 2009. *Trade statistics in policymaking: a handbook of commonly used trade indices and indicators*. United Nations publication. Available at: https://www.unescap.org/resources/trade-statistics-policymaking-handbook-commonly-used-trade-indeces-and-indicators-revised. Accessed on August 20, 2019.

Mulualem, Melaku. 2014. *America coming to Africa: a comparison with China.* Available at: <https://media.africaportal.org/documents/attachment-51-America_is_coming_to_Africa_a_comparison_with_China.pdf. Accessed October 26, 2020.

Mutambara, Tsitsi E. 2017. "How has trade between South Africa and China evolved over the past decade?" *Transnational Corporation Review*, 9(2): 97-111. Accessed on December 25, 2017. DOI: 10.1080/19186444.2017.1326721 http://dx.doi.org/10.1080/19186444.2017.1326721.

Mutambara, Tsitsi E. 2016. "How important is Africa as China's trading partner? A comparison with China's other trading partners." *Fort Hare Papers. Multidisciplinary Journal of the University of Fort Hare.* Volume 22, 2016. ISBN: 978-1-86810-736-0. Pages 51-68.

Mutambara, Tsitsi E. 2013a. "Examining India, Brazil and South Africa (IBSA) trade: Trade intensity, Comparative advantages and Intra-industry trade opportunities." *Journal of Business and Policy Research (JBPR)*. 8(3):17-39.

Mutambara, Tsitsi E. 2013b. "Africa-Asia trade versus Africa's trade with the North: Trends and trajectories." *African Review of Economics and Finance*. 4(2):273-299.

Mutambara, Tsitsi E. 2010. "Examining South-South trade flows and market access conditions: A case study of India, Brazil and South Africa Development Initiative." *TIPS Working Paper Series*. Accessible at: http://www.tips.org.za/publication/examining-south-south-trade-flows-and-market-access-conditions-case-study-india-brazil-a Accessed on December 30, 2010.

Office of the United States Trade Representative. 2019a. *U.S. Generalized System of Preferences-Guidebook.* Available at: https://ustr.gov/sites/default/files/IssueAreas/gsp/GSP_Guidebook-December_2019.pdf. Accessed on January 18, 2021.

Office of the United States Trade Representative. 2019b. *Trade and Investment Framework Agreements.* Available at: https://ustr.gov/trade-agreements/trade-investment-framework-agreements. Accessed on January 18, 2021.

Office of the United States Trade Representative. 2020. "AGOA eligible and ineligible countries-2020." In *2020 Biennial Report on the Implementation of the African Growth and Opportunity Act* (June 2020). Available at: https://ustr.gov/sites/default/files/assets/agoa/USTR-Biennial-Report-to-Congress-on-AGOA-062320.pdf Accessed on January 18, 2021.

Olander, Eric C. 2020a."How China finances all that infrastructure construction in Africa is starting to change. Here is how." *The China Africa Project*. Available at: https://chinaafricaproject.com/analysis/china-africa-101-the-new-china-africa-swap-financing-model/ Accessed on April 23, 2021.

Olander, Eric C. 2020b."China's infrastructure finance model is changing. Here is how." *The Africa Report*. Available at: https://www.theafricareport.com/22133/chinas-infrastructure-finance-model-is-changing-heres-how/ Accessed on April 23, 2021.

People's Republic of China State Council, 2010. *China-Africa Economic And Trade Cooperation. A White Paper, December 2010*. Available: https://china.usc.edu/prc-state-council-china-africa-economic-and-trade-cooperation-december-2010 Accessed on March 18, 2016.

Pigato, Miria and Wenxia Tang. 2015. "China and Africa: Expanding Economic Ties in an Evolving Global Context." *World Bank Group Investing in Africa Forum, Working paper*. Addis Ababa, Ethiopia. Available at: https://www.worldbank.org/content/dam/Worldbank/Event/Africa/Investing%20in%20Africa%20Forum/2015/investing-in-africa-forum-china-and-africa-expanding-economic-ties-in-an-evolving-global-context.pdf. Accessed on April 22, 2021.

Sandrey, Ron and Hannah Edinder. 2011. "China's manufacturing and industrialisation in Africa." *African Development Bank Group Working Paper Series*. Working paper no.128.

Scholvin, Sören and Jöran Wrana. 2015. "From the Cape to Cairo: The Potential of the Tripartite Free Trade Area" *SAIIA Occasional Paper* 221. Available: https://0-www.africaportal.org.wam.seals.ac.za/publications/from-the-cape-to-cairo-the-potential-of-the-tripartite-free-trade-area/ Accessed on February 13, 2019.

Statistics South Africa. 2018. *BRICS: Where does South Africa rank?* Available at: http://www.statssa.gov.za/?p=11355&gclid=EAIaIQobChMIuOOUxJXJ7wIVCertCh0-mAfGEAAYASAAEgLfhfD_BwE Accessed on March 24, 2021.

Subasat, Turan. 2003. "What does Heckscher-Ohlin model contribute to international trade theory? A critical assessment." *Review of Radical*

Political Economy. 35(2): 148-165. https://journals.sagepub.com/doi/10.1177/048661340303500200З Accessed on March 24, 2019.

Tiezzi, Shannon. 2015. *China, Egypt consolidate ties after Sisi's attendance at military parade*. Available at: https://thediplomat.com/2015/09/china-egypt-consolidate-ties-after-sisis-attendance-at-military-parade/ Accessed on March 16, 2021.

Trade and Industrial Policy Strategies (TIPS). 2019. *Trade performance indicators*. Available: http://www.tips.org.za/files/basic_templates/Trade%20Indicator%20Guide.pdf Accessed on January 18, 2021.

Trade Law Centre (TRALAC). 2015. *Trade policy review: Angola*. Available at: https://www.tralac.org/news/article/8122-trade-policy-review-angola.html Accessed November 3, 2020.

United Nations Conference on Trade and Development (UNCTAD) and World Trade Organisation (WTO). 2012. *A Practical Guide to Trade Policy Analysis*. World Trade Organisation and United Nations Conference on Trade and Development. Geneva, Switzerland.

United Nations Conference on Trade and Development (UNCTAD), 2018. *Generalised System of Preferences – List of Beneficiaries*. (UNCTAD/ITCD/TSB/Misc.62/Rev.7) United Nations New York and Geneva. Available: https://unctad.org/system/files/official-document/itcdtsbmisc62rev7_en.pdf Accessed on January 18, 2021.

US Department of State. 2021. *US relations with Egypt*. Available at: https://www.state.gov/u-s-relations-with-egypt/#:~:text=Total%20two%2Dway%20trade%20in,%2C%20textiles%2C%20and%20agricultural%20products. Accessed on March 16, 2021.

US Department of State. 2021. *U.S. relations with Algeria*. Available at: https://www.state.gov/u-s-relations-with-algeria/ Accessed on March 22, 2021.

US Embassy in Algeria. 2017. *US-Algeria relations*. Available at https://dz.usembassy.gov/u-s-algeria-relations/ Accessed on March 22, 2021.

Vahalik, Bohdan. 2014. "Regional bilateral trade analysis of the European Union, China and ASEAN." *Procedia Economics and Finance*. 12

(2014): 709-717. Available: https://www.sciencedirect.com/science/article/pii/S2212567114003979 Accessed on January 20, 2020.

Viljoen, Willemien. 2019. "The China-Africa trade relationship." *Tralac Trade Brief No. S19TB22/2019*. Trade Law Centre (Tralac).

Willcox, Owen and Dirk van Seventer. 2005. "Current and potential trade between South Africa and China." In *Enter the Dragon: Towards a free trade agreement between China and the Southern African Customs Union*, edited by Peter Draper and Garth le Pere, Pages 167-220. Institute for Global Dialogue, Midrand, South Africa and The South African Institute of International Affairs, Johannesburg.

World Integrated Trade Solution (WITS). 2018. *Trade Indicators.* Available: https://wits.worldbank.org/wits/wits/witshelp/Content/Utilities/e1.trade_indicators.htm Accessed on November 19, 2018.

Wright, George. 2001. "The Clinton administration's policy toward Angola: an assessment. *Review of African Political Economy*." *28*(90): 563-576.

World Trade Organisation Committee on Trade and Development (WTCOMTD). 2011a. *China's duty-free quota-free programme for LDC products.* WT/COMTD/N/39/Add.1/Rev.1. Available: http://G/C/W/656/Rev.1-WT/COMTD/N/39/Add.1/Rev.1) Accessed on January 14, 2021.

World Trade Organisation Committee on Trade and Development (WTCOMTD). 2011b. *Notification of Preferential Trade Arrangement.* WT/COMTD/N/39. Available: http://WT/COMTD/N/39 Accessed on January 14, 2021.

World Trade Organisation (WTO). 2016. *Duty-free treatment for least developed countries-China.* Available: http://ptadb.wto.org/docs/China_LDC/2016/En-Annex%201.%20DF%20TREATMENT%20FOR%20LDCs%20-%20CHINA.pdf. Accessed on January 14, 2021.

Zoubir, Yahia. 2011. "The United States and Algeria: A New Strategic Partnership?" *Journal of Middle Eastern and Islamic Studies (in Asia).* 5(4): 1-27. Accessed February 26, 2021. DOI: 10.1080/19370679.2011.12023188.

Appendices

Table A-1. A comparison between China-Africa trade and USA-Africa trade (2001-2020)

The top 20 major products	**Period of years**																			
	2001	2002	2003	2004	2005	2006	2007	2008	2009	2010	2011	2012	2013	2014	2015	2016	2017	2018	2019	2020
Total trade with Africa (US$ billion)																				
China-Africa trade	8.2	9.4	14.9	20.5	29.0	41.1	63.5	91.7	84.9	112	131	148	151	149	133	115	131	164	170	51.8
USA-Africa trade	31.8	29.3	40.7	50.7	69.0	84.2	101	131	75.5	109	129	99.3	71.2	63.6	49.7	50.5	51.9	55.1	53.3	22.5
Percentage (%) share of Africa's total trade (Africa's world trade)																				
China-Africa trade	3.5	4.0	5.0	6.2	7.2	7.5	8.8	10.4	11.1	11.7	11.5	12.8	13.7	13.3	14.5	13.3	14.5	15.2	16.3	48.6
USA-Africa trade	13.9	12.5	13.9	15.3	17.2	15.4	14.0	14.8	9.9	11.4	11.3	8.6	6.5	5.7	5.4	5.8	5.8	5.1	5.1	12.4
Trade balances with Africa (US$ billion)																				
China-Africa trade	-0.7	-1.4	-7.9	-3.3	-5.1	-6.7	0.3	4.6	-4.3	-2.8	0.7	8.1	-4.2	-17.5	-37.0	-42.5	-26.4	-19.9	-30.5	-4.0
USA-Africa trade	10.9	8.5	17.1	26.2	40.2	47.3	52.0	75.1	26.6	41.8	45.9	31.4	6.0	-7.8	-8.7	-3.6	1.1	-1.4	-6.0	-2.5
Percentage (%) share of Africa's total trade (Africa's world trade) by Africa's top 15 trading countries																				
USA-Africa trade	13.9	12.5	13.8	15.3	17.2	15.4	14.0	14.8	9.9	11.4	11.3	8.6	6.5	5.7	5.4	5.8	5.8	5.1	5.1	12.4
France-Africa trade	12.1	12.0	11.5	11.9	10.8	8.9	7.7	7.9	7.7	6.7	6.5	6.2	6.4	6.0	5.8	5.7	5.6	5.5	5.5	13.6
Italy-Africa trade	9.8	9.5	9.1	9.5	9.8	8.6	6.7	7.8	5.7	6.3	5.4	6.4	5.9	5.0	4.7	4.9	4.7	4.8	4.1	9.5

Table A-1. (Continued)

The top 20	Period of years																			
major products	2001	2002	2003	2004	2005	2006	2007	2008	2009	2010	2011	2012	2013	2014	2015	2016	2017	2018	2019	2020
Germany-Africa trade	7.6	7.2	6.9	7.4	7.4	6.0	4.9	4.7	4.3	3.9	3.9	4.0	4.3	4.1	4.5	4.5	4.7	3.9	4.3	11.0
UK-Africa trade	7.1	6.8	6.5	6.5	5.9	4.9	3.8	3.8	3.3	3.0	3.6	4.2	4.1	3.3	2.8	2.7	2.6	2.7	2.4	5.1
S. Africa-Africa trade	4.7	5.5	5.1	5.5	4.8	4.1	4.1	4.0	4.8	4.1	4.5	4.9	4.7	4.4	4.3	4.2	4.1	3.8	3.6	7.6
Spain-Africa trade	5.4	5.6	5.7	6.2	6.6	5.7	3.9	4.7	4.0	3.7	3.8	4.3	4.9	4.9	4.7	4.7	4.9	4.7	4.6	10.4
China-Africa trade	3.5	4.0	5.0	6.2	7.2	7.5	8.8	10.4	11.1	11.7	11.5	12.8	13.7	13.3	14.5	13.3	14.5	15.2	16.3	48.6
India-Africa trade	2.5	2.9	2.5	1.9	2.3	3.4	3.5	3.8	3.8	4.3	4.7	5.3	5.5	5.6	5.5	5.0	5.6	5.4	5.9	5.7
Netherlands-Africa	3.5	3.7	3.6	3.9	4.2	3.3	3.0	3.7	3.1	3.1	3.0	3.5	3.9	3.8	3.3	2.9	3.0	3.0	2.8	8.4
Japan-Africa trade	3.7	4.1	4.1	4.5	4.3	3.7	3.7	3.3	2.8	2.7	2.7	2.9	2.7	2.5	2.3	2.0	1.9	1.7	1.8	4.2
Belgium-Africa trade	3.0	3.2	2.6	2.6	2.9	2.4	2.9	2.0	1.8	1.9	1.8	1.9	2.0	2.1	2.1	2.3	2.3	2.1	2.1	5.9
S. Korea-Africa trade	2.2	2.1	1.9	2.2	2.2	2.5	1.7	1.8	2.1	2.2	2.0	1.6	2.0	1.9	1.8	2.2	1.6	1.8	1.5	3.8
Turkey-Africa trade	1.5	1.5	1.5	1.9	2.1	1.7	1.2	1.4	1.7	1.5	1.5	1.7	1.9	2.0	2.1	2.1	2.1	2.0	2.2	6.6
Switzerland-Africa	1.6	1.4	1.7	1.7	1.9	1.6	1.2	1.3	1.5	1.5	1.8	1.8	2.0	1.7	1.7	1.8	1.7	1.6	1.6	4.7

Source: Own tables constructed using statistical data from the International Trade Centre trade database available at http://www.trademap.org.

Table A-2. China's major trading partners in Africa

African countries	Period of years																		
	2001	2002	2003	2004	2005	2006	2007	2008	2009	2010	2011	2012	2013	2014	2015	2016	2017	2018	2019
South Africa	1st	1st	1st	1st	1st	2nd	2nd	2nd	2nd	1st	1st	1st	1st	1st	1st	1st	1st	1st	1st
Angola	4th	3rd	2nd	2nd	2nd	1st	1st	1st	1st	2nd	2nd	2nd	2nd	2nd	2nd	2nd	2nd	2nd	2nd
Nigeria	2nd	2nd	3rd	3rd	3rd	4th	4th	3rd	3rd	3rd	3rd	3rd	3rd	3rd	3rd	4th	3rd	3rd	3rd
Egypt	3rd	4th	4th	4th	4th	3rd	3rd	4th	4th	4th	4th	4th	4th	4th	4th	3rd	4th	4th	4th
Algeria	5th	5th	5th	5th	5th	5th	5th	5th	5th	5th	5th	5th	5th	5th	5th	5th	5th	5th	5th
Percentage (%) share of China's total trade with Africa																			
All 5 countries	50.0	50.8	53.8	53.9	52.9	54.4	55.8	57.3	55.5	55.5	59.7	63.2	63.4	61.3	57.0	54.1	55.3	53.8	52.1
The five countries total trade with China (US$ billion) and growth (%)																			
South Africa	2.22	2.58	3.87	5.91	7.27	9.85	14.1	17.9	16.1	25.7	45.5	60.0	65.2	60.3	46.1	35.5	39.7	43.6	42.5
% growth rate	45.17%					34.09%					-12.29%					2.24%			
Angola	0.77	1.15	2.35	4.91	6.95	11.8	14.1	25.3	17.1	24.8	27.7	37.6	35.9	37.1	19.7	15.6	22.7	27.9	25.4
% growth rate	98.13%					18.35%					-19.76%					3.78%			
Nigeria	1.14	1.17	1.86	2.18	2.83	3.13	4.34	7.28	6.37	7.77	10.8	10.6	13.6	18.0	15.0	11.0	13.8	15.4	19.3
% growth rate	28.60%					25.59%					0.94%					11.57%			
Egypt	0.95	0.94	1.09	1.58	2.15	3.19	4.71	6.30	5.86	6.96	8.80	9.54	10.2	11.6	12.9	11.1	10.8	13.9	13.2
% growth rate	35.27%					16.93%					3.96%					6.73%			
Algeria	0.29	0.43	0.75	1.24	1.77	2.09	3.90	4.60	5.13	5.18	6.43	7.73	8.19	8.71	8.38	8.07	7.24	9.10	8.09
% growth rate	63.55%					13.31%					1.09%					3.73%			
The five countries trade balances with China (US$ billion)																			
South Africa	0.12	-0.1	-0.2	0.01	-0.4	-1.7	-0.8	0.62	1.33	4.10	18.7	29.3	31.6	28.9	14.3	9.62	9.94	10.9	9.37
Angola	0.68	1.03	2.06	4.52	6.21	10.0	11.7	19.4	12.3	20.8	22.1	29.5	28.0	25.1	12.3	12.2	18.1	23.4	21.3
Nigeria	-0.7	-0.9	-1.7	-1.3	-1.8	-2.6	-3.3	-6.3	-4.6	-5.6	-7.6	-8.0	-11	-13	-12	-9.2	-11	-12	-14
Egypt	-0.8	-0.8	-0.8	-1.2	-1.7	-2.8	-4.2	-5.4	-4.4	-5.1	-5.8	-6.9	-6.5	-9.3	-11	-10	-8.2	-10	-11
Algeria	-0.2	-0.3	-0.5	-0.7	-1.0	-1.8	-1.6	-2.9	-3.2	-2.8	-2.5	-3.1	-3.9	-6.1	-6.8	-7.4	-6.3	-6.7	-5.8

Source: Own tables constructed using statistical data from the International Trade Centre trade database available at http://www.trademap.org.

Table A-3. USA's major trading partners in Africa

African countries	Period of years																		
	2001	2002	2003	2004	2005	2006	2007	2008	2009	2010	2011	2012	2013	2014	2015	2016	2017	2018	2019
Nigeria	1st	1st	1st	1st	1st	1st	1st	1st	1st	1st	1st	1st	1st	2nd	3rd	2nd	2nd	2nd	3rd
South Africa	2nd	2nd	2nd	2nd	3rd	4th	3rd	4th	4th	3rd	2nd	2nd	2nd	1st	1st	1st	1st	1st	1st
Egypt	3rd	3rd	5th	5th	5th	5th	5th	5th	5th	5th	5th	5th	4th	3rd	2nd	4th	3rd	3rd	2nd
Algeria	4th	5th	3rd	3rd	2nd	2nd	2nd	3rd	2nd	2nd	3rd	3rd	5th	5th	4th	3rd	4th	4th	4th
Angola	5th	4th	4th	4th	4th	3rd	4th	2nd	3rd	4th	4th	4th	3rd	4th	5th	5th	5th	5th	5th
Percentage (%) share of the USA's total trade with Africa																			
All 5 countries	76.4	75.1	76.5	76.0	76.7	78.8	78.7	76.3	72.7	76.2	75.6	71.7	67.4	65.2	63.8	66.2	64.9	63.0	60.7
The five countries total trade with the USA (US$ billion) and growth (%)																			
South Africa	7.39	6.70	7.61	9.33	9.99	12.2	14.8	16.6	10.4	14.0	16.9	16.4	15.9	14.8	13.0	11.6	13.0	14.2	13.3
% growth rate	7.84%					3.49%					-6.42%					4.76%			
Angola	3.37	3.66	5.00	5.39	9.78	13.7	14.2	21.6	11.1	13.6	15.3	11.5	10.4	7.88	4.08	4.23	3.50	3.29	1.52
% growth rate	30.49%					-0.29%					-28.17%					-28.64%			
Nigeria	9.73	7.26	12.0	18.7	26.8	31.2	36.5	43.3	23.4	35.4	39.4	24.4	18.4	9.90	5.44	6.27	9.49	8.45	7.94
% growth rate	28.80%					3.23%					-39.04%					8.11%			
Egypt	4.44	4.29	3.83	4.47	5.38	6.68	7.89	8.52	7.43	9.19	8.39	8.61	6.87	7.95	6.24	5.05	5.71	7.63	8.78
% growth rate	4.88%					8.31%					-7.14%					20.06%			
Algeria	3.74	3.54	5.61	8.90	12.0	17.2	20.1	21.3	12.3	16.1	16.5	11.6	6.81	7.41	5.41	5.61	5.05	6.04	3.59
% growth rate	33.95%					-1.57%					-24.33%					-13.68%			
The five countries trade balances with the USA (US$ billion)																			
South Africa	1.47	1.65	1.97	2.98	2.18	3.27	3.76	3.64	2.51	2.73	2.35	1.28	1.29	2.10	2.04	2.37	2.90	3.15	2.65
Angola	2.82	2.91	4.02	4.20	7.92	10.6	11.6	17.4	8.28	11.0	12.3	8.54	7.48	3.80	1.75	1.73	1.88	2.24	0.45
Nigeria	7.82	5.14	9.93	15.6	23.5	26.7	31.0	35.1	16.1	27.3	29.6	14.4	5.60	-2.0	-1.4	2.48	5.14	3.08	1.58
Egypt	-2.7	-1.4	-1.4	-1.7	-0.9	-1.5	-2.8	-3.5	-.3.1	-4.5	-4.1	-2.4	-3.5	-5.0	-3.3	-1.9	-2.3	-2.5	-2.2
Algeria	1.66	1.57	4.63	6.95	9.83	15.0	16.8	18.8	10.0	13.7	13.3	8.84	3.11	2.18	1.66	1.23	2.93	3.52	1.59

Source: Own tables constructed using statistical data from the International Trade Centre trade database available at http://www.trademap.org.

Table A-4. A comparison of China and USA as major import sources and export destinations for the major trading partners in Africa

	Period of years																		
	2001	2002	2003	2004	2005	2006	2007	2008	2009	2010	2011	2012	2013	2014	2015	2016	2017	2018	2019
Rank as a major import source for Algeria																			
China	n/a	n/a	6th	5th	3rd	3rd	3rd	3rd	2nd	2nd	2nd	2nd	1st	1st	1st	1st	1st	--	--
USA	3rd	2nd	5th	6th	3rd	5th	4th	6th	6th	6th	6th	7th	6th	6th	6th	6th	7th	--	--
Rank as a major export destination for Algeria																			
China	n/a	n/a	n/a	n/a	n/a	n/a	n/a	n/a	n/a	n/a	n/a	n/a	n/a	n/a	n/a	n/a	n/a	--	--
USA	1st	1st	1st	1st	1st	1st	1st	1st	1st	1st	1st	2nd	4th	4th	4th	4th	4th	--	--
Rank as a major import source for Angola																			
China	--	--	--	4th	4th	3rd	3rd	--	2nd	2nd	2nd	2nd	2nd	2nd	2nd	2nd	2nd	1st	1st
USA	--	--	--	2nd	2nd	2nd	2nd	--	3rd	3rd	4th	3rd	4th	3rd	3rd	3rd	3rd	4th	6th
Rank as a major export destination for Angola																			
China	--	--	--	n/a	n/a	2nd	1st	--	1st	1st	1st	1st	1st	1st	1st	1st	1st	1st	1st
USA	--	--	--	2nd	n/a	1st	2nd	--	2nd	2nd	2nd	3rd	3rd	4th	4th	3rd	4th	3rd	6th
Rank as a major import source for Egypt																			
China	4th	3rd	3rd	3rd	3rd	3rd	4th	2nd	2nd	2nd	2nd	1st	1st	1st	1st	1st	1st	1st	1st
USA	1st	1st	1st	1st	1st	1st	1st	1st	1st	1st	1st	2nd	3rd	3rd	3rd	3rd	4th	3rd	2nd
Rank as a major export destination for Egypt																			
China	n/a	n/a	n/a	n/a	n/a	n/a	n/a	n/a	n/a	n/a	n/a	n/a	n/a	n/a	n/a	n/a	n/a	n/a	n/a
USA	2nd	3rd	2nd	2nd	2nd	3rd	3rd	3rd	1st	3rd	4th	3rd	5th	5th	4th	5th	5th	4th	1st
Rank as a major import source for Nigeria																			
China	4th	4th	4th	--	--	2nd	1st	1st	1st	2nd	2nd	1st	1st	1st	1st	1st	1st	1st	1st
USA	2nd	1st	1st	--	--	1st	2nd	2nd	2nd	1st	1st	2nd	2nd	2nd	2nd	2nd	2nd	4th	4th
Rank as a major export destination for Nigeria																			
China	n/a	n/a	9th	--	--	n/a	6th	9th	8th	8th	8th	5th	10th	9th	9th	9th	9th	7th	10th

Table A-4. (Continued)

	Period of years																		
	2001	2002	2003	2004	2005	2006	2007	2008	2009	2010	2011	2012	2013	2014	2015	2016	2017	2018	2019
USA	1st	1st	1st	--	--	1st	1st	1st	1st	1st	1st	1st	3rd	8th	6th	2nd	2nd	6th	9th
Rank as a major import source for South Africa																			
China	5th	4th	4th	3rd	2nd	2nd	2nd	1st	1st	1st	1st	1st	1st	1st	1st	1st	1st	1st	1st
USA	3rd	3rd	3rd	3rd	3rd	3rd	3rd	3rd	3rd	3rd	3rd	3rd	3rd	3rd	3rd	3rd	3rd	3rd	3rd
Rank as a major export destination for South Africa																			
China	6th	6th	6th	6th	6th	6th	5th	5th	1st	1st	1st	1st	1st	1st	1st	1st	1st	1st	1st
USA	1st	1st	1st	1st	1st	1st	1st	1st	2nd	2nd	2nd	2nd	2nd	2nd	2nd	2nd	2nd	3rd	3rd

Source: Own tables constructed using statistical data from the International Trade Centre trade database available at http://www.trademap.org.

Notes: n/a = not among the top ten countries. -- = statistical data were not available.

Table A-5. A comparison of the trade shares of China and USA in the world trade of major trading partners in Africa

	Period of years																		
	2001	2002	2003	2004	2005	2006	2007	2008	2009	2010	2011	2012	2013	2014	2015	2016	2017	2018	2019
Percentage (%) share of total trade with Algeria in Algeria's world trade																			
China - Algeria	0.97	1.36	1.59	2.31	2.42	2.26	3.98	3.85	6.66	5.89	5.73	7.00	7.45	8.38	10.2	11.3	11.1	--	--
USA - Algeria	12.7	12.2	14.7	17.2	18.0	21.4	23.0	17.8	14.7	16.3	14.3	10.3	6.38	6.44	5.72	8.02	6.54	--	--
Percentage (%) share of total trade with Angola in Angola's world trade																			
China - Angola	--	--	--	3.49	5.00	10.43	25.9	--	28.0	32.2	30.0	37.3	36.8	35.4	38.2	36.8	43.0	45.3	47.8
USA - Angola	--	--	--	10.2	7.95	13.9	21.5	--	15.0	16.5	20.9	9.05	7.09	5.54	4.86	7.61	4.22	4.06	3.24
Percentage (%) share of total trade with Egypt in Egypt's world trade																			

	Period of years																		
	2001	2002	2003	2004	2005	2006	2007	2008	2009	2010	2011	2012	2013	2014	2015	2016	2017	2018	2019
China - Egypt	3.28	4.55	3.73	3.82	3.36	3.80	4.08	6.06	7.07	6.72	6.75	7.39	7.92	8.55	10.6	10.1	9.45	11.4	11.5
USA - Egypt	12.9	12.1	10.5	9.45	8.95	8.16	8.12	8.80	9.23	8.20	8.83	7.34	6.70	6.45	5.82	5.29	5.67	6.49	6.80
Percentage (%) share of total trade with Nigeria in Nigeria's world trade																			
China - Nigeria	2.51	2.97	3.06	--	--	3.85	6.70	4.15	8.01	6.70	6.32	8.80	7.98	7.95	10.5	10.7	8.67	8.91	13.6
USA - Nigeria	31.3	25.4	29.6	--	--	36.8	34.8	33.7	18.7	28.8	21.0	16.2	8.56	8.82	5.71	10.0	10.8	6.60	7.43
Percentage (%) share of total trade with South Africa in South Africa's world trade																			
China–S Africa	2.96	3.67	4.69	5.27	6.19	7.42	8.85	8.80	11.9	11.8	12.7	12.3	14.1	12.6	13.8	13.4	13.8	13.7	14.5
USA - S Africa	12.9	11.2	111.0	10.0	9.06	9.31	9.52	9.30	8.34	7.95	7.67	7.54	6.79	6.80	7.33	6.96	7.06	6.35	6.77

Source: Own tables constructed using statistical data from the International Trade Centre trade database available at http://www.trademap.org.

Table A-6. Types of the top 20 major products imported (in order of value) from Africa by the USA and China

Period of years			
	2001 2002 2003 2004 2005 2006 2007 2008	2009 2010	2011 2012 2013 2014 2015 2016 2017 2018 2019 2020
Product code (HS-2 digit)	Imported by the United States of America	Product code (HS-2 digit)	Imported by China
	Product classification by factor intensity [skill & technology intensity]		Product classification by factor intensity [skill & technology intensity]
HS27	Mineral fuels	HS27	Mineral fuels
HS71	Non-fuel primary commodities; very few Resource-intensive manufactures	HS26	Non-fuel primary commodities; very few Resource-intensive manufactures
HS62	Resource-intensive manufactures	HS74	Mainly Non-fuel primary commodities; few Low skill- & technology-intensive manufactures
HS26	Non-fuel primary commodities; very few Mineral fuels	HS81	Mainly Non-fuel primary commodities; few Low skill- & technology-intensive manufactures

Table A-6. (Continued)

Period of years																				
	2001	2002	2003	2004	2005	2006	2007	2008	2009	2010	2011	2012	2013	2014	2015	2016	2017	2018	2019	2020
HS61	Resource-intensive manufactures								HS44		Mainly Resource-intensive manufactures; few Non-fuel primary commodities									
HS18	Non-fuel primary commodities								HS12		Non-fuel primary commodities									
HS72	Low skill- and technology-intensive manufactures								HS72		Low skill-and technology-intensive manufactures									
HS84	Mainly Medium skill-and technology-intensive manufactures; some High skill-and technology-intensive manufactures; very few Low skill-and technology-intensive manufactures								HS52		Mainly Resource-intensive manufactures; very few Non-fuel primary commodities									
HS09	Non-fuel primary commodities								HS51		Mainly Resource-intensive manufactures; very few Non-fuel primary commodities									
HS87	Medium skill-and technology-intensive manufactures; Low skill- and technology-intensive manufactures; very few Resource-intensive manufactures								HS25		Non-fuel primary commodities; very few Resource-intensive manufactures									
HS76	Mainly Non-fuel primary commodities; some Low skill- and technology-intensive manufactures								HS03		Non-fuel primary commodities									
HS08	Non-fuel primary commodities								HS18		Non-fuel primary commodities									
HS29	High skill-and technology-intensive manufactures								HS71		Non-fuel primary commodities; very few Resource-intensive manufactures									
HS85	Mainly Medium skill-and technology-intensive manufactures; some High skill-and technology-intensive manufactures; very few Low skill-and technology-intensive manufactures								HS47		Non-fuel primary commodities									

<table>
<tr><th colspan="21">Period of years</th></tr>
<tr><th></th><th>2001</th><th>2002</th><th>2003</th><th>2004</th><th>2005</th><th>2006</th><th>2007</th><th>2008</th><th>2009</th><th>2010</th><th>2011</th><th>2012</th><th>2013</th><th>2014</th><th>2015</th><th>2016</th><th>2017</th><th>2018</th><th>2019</th><th>2020</th></tr>
<tr><td>HS40</td><td colspan="8">Mainly Medium skill-and technology-intensive manufactures; few Non-fuel primary commodities</td><td colspan="2">HS39</td><td colspan="10">Mainly High skill-and technology-intensive manufactures; some Medium skill-and technology-intensive manufactures</td></tr>
<tr><td>HS28</td><td colspan="8">High skill-and technology-intensive manufactures</td><td colspan="2">HS75</td><td colspan="10">Non-fuel primary commodities; very few Low skill-and technology-intensive manufactures</td></tr>
<tr><td>HS25</td><td colspan="8">Non-fuel primary commodities; very few Resource-intensive manufactures</td><td colspan="2">HS41</td><td colspan="10">Mainly Resource-intensive manufactures; some Non-fuel primary commodities</td></tr>
<tr><td>HS57</td><td colspan="8">Resource-intensive manufactures</td><td colspan="2">HS84</td><td colspan="10">Mainly Medium skill-and technology-intensive manufactures; some High skill-and technology-intensive manufactures; very few Low skill-and technology-intensive manufactures</td></tr>
<tr><td>HS15</td><td colspan="8">Non-fuel primary commodities</td><td colspan="2">HS24</td><td colspan="10">Non-fuel primary commodities</td></tr>
<tr><td>HS03</td><td colspan="8">Non-fuel primary commodities</td><td colspan="2">HS29</td><td colspan="10">High skill-and technology-intensive manufactures</td></tr>
</table>

Source: Own tables constructed using statistical data from the International Trade Centre trade database available at http://www.trademap.org.

Table A-7. Trade shares (%) by the top 20 major products imported from Africa by the USA to total imports from Africa (2001-2019)

The top 20 major products	Period of years																		
	2001	2002	2003	2004	2005	2006	2007	2008	2009	2010	2011	2012	2013	2014	2015	2016	2017	2018	2019
HS27 Mineral fuels	73.7	74.9	76.0	78.5	84.2	85.1	85.8	87.2	81.2	82.0	81.5	76.7	65.6	53.1	34.5	47.9	48.9	47.5	40.3
Non-fuel primary commodities	11.3	6.5	8.6	7.7	6.8	6.7	7.3	5.1	6.9	6.7	6.4	8.1	13.2	17.1	25.1	19.2	20.6	22.6	25.3
Resource-intensive & low-skill & tech-intensive manuf.	5.5	6.9	6.5	6.4	3.6	3.1	2.1	2.2	3.7	2.9	2.9	3.7	5.5	9.5	10.7	9.9	10.3	9.9	12.1
High Value Added manuf. products	5.0	6.5	4.9	3.9	3.0	2.7	2.8	3.6	5.6	5.2	6.4	6.8	9.5	11.4	14.9	11.9	9.9	7.9	9.0
All top 20 products	95.5	94.9	96.0	96.5	97.6	97.6	98.1	98.1	97.4	96.8	97.3	95.3	93.9	91.0	85.3	89.0	89.7	87.9	86.7
Percentage (%) share of total imports from Africa																			
High skill technology intensive manufactures	2.1	2.2	2.0	1.5	1.4	1.1	1.4	1.5	1.4	1.6	1.9	2.4	3.1	4.5	5.7	5.4	5.1	6.2	7.4
Medium skill technology intensive manufactures	2.5	2.8	1.9	2.2	1.8	1.2	1.2	1.7	2.2	2.0	2.6	3.3	4.4	5.0	7.2	6.8	4.6	3.8	4.4
Total for high value added manufactures	4.6	5.0	3.9	3.7	3.2	2.3	2.6	3.2	3.6	3.6	4.5	5.7	7.6	9.5	12.9	12.2	9.7	10.0	11.8

Source: Own tables constructed using statistical data from the International Trade Centre trade database available at http://www.trademap.org.

Table A-8. Trade shares (%) by the top 20 major products imported from Africa by China to total imports from Africa (2001-2019)

The top 20 major products	Period of years																		
	2001	2002	2003	2004	2005	2006	2007	2008	2009	2010	2011	2012	2013	2014	2015	2016	2017	2018	2019
HS27 Mineral fuels	73.3	69.0	74.1	68.3	72.1	71.5	82.3	81.7	73.9	69.5	67.4	73.0	69.4	71.9	67.1	58.3	62.9	64.9	61.4
Non-fuel primary commodities	11.4	11.8	8.5	14.8	14.1	16.9	10.0	13.1	18.2	23.1	25.2	20.3	24.8	22.0	24.8	31.2	29.7	28.8	32.0
Resource-intensive & low-skill & tech-intensive manuf.	10.0	11.5	12.2	11.8	9.5	8.4	5.7	3.3	5.0	5.0	3.8	3.4	4.0	4.2	5.7	7.4	4.8	4.1	4.1
High Value Added manuf. products	2.3	0.9	1.3	1.6	1.3	0.9	0.7	0.6	0.7	0.7	0.5	0.5	0.5	0.5	0.3	0.4	0.4	0.3	0.4
All top 20 products	96.9	93.2	96.2	96.5	97.0	97.7	98.8	98.8	97.8	98.3	96.9	97.2	98.7	98.5	97.9	97.3	97.8	98.2	97.9
Percentage (%) share of total imports from Africa																			
High skill technology intensive manufactures	4.1	3.7	2.9	2.1	1.9	1.7	1.5	1.2	1.4	1.4	0.8	0.7	0.7	0.7	0.9	1.1	1.0	1.0	1.0
Medium skill technology intensive manufactures	2.2	1.5	1.7	1.3	1.1	1.1	1.0	0.6	0.6	0.6	0.5	0.4	0.5	0.4	05	0.6	0.5	0.4	0.5
Total for high value added manufactures	6.3	5.2	4.6	3.4	3.0	2.8	2.4	1.8	2.0	2.0	1.3	1.1	1.2	1.1	1.4	1.7	1.5	1.4	1.5

Source: Own tables constructed using statistical data from the International Trade Centre trade database available at http://www.trademap.org.

Table A-9. Major imports by the USA and China from the top 5 African countries

	Period of years																		
	2001	2002	2003	2004	2005	2006	2007	2008	2009	2010	2011	2012	2013	2014	2015	2016	2017	2018	2019
Percentage (%) share of HS 27 (Mineral fuels) in total imports from Algeria																			
China - Algeria	94.4	89.0	73.4	99.7	99.5	97.0	99.7	99.6	98.6	99.2	99.6	99.8	99.8	99.5	99.1	96.9	97.8	98.4	99.5
USA - Algeria	98.5	99.5	98.8	99.7	99.8	99.9	99.7	99.7	99.9	99.9	99.9	99.9	99.8	98.9	96.7	95.0	97.4	96.4	90.9
Percentage (%) share of HS 27 (Mineral fuels) in total imports from Angola																			
China - Angola	…	…	…	…	…	…	99.5	…	99.3	99.8	99.8	100	100	100	99.8	99.8	99.8	99.9	…
USA - Angola	…	…	…	95.0	..	96.5	100	…	99.7	100	100	100	99.9	99.9	94.0	93.9	96.6	75.3	…
Percentage (%) share of HS 27 (Mineral fuels) in total imports from Nigeria																			
China - Nigeria	100	98.1	88.9	…	…	…	84.1	54.9	76.1	48.3	45.1	79.7	77.4	90.5	81.9	85.2	81.6	78.7	92.5
USA - Nigeria	99.8	99.6	97.7	..	..	99.3	99.4	98.9	98.9	95.8	95.3	92.4	92.7	91.3	59.6	99.4	98.8	98.7	96.7
Percentage (%) share of major imports by China from Egypt (in total imports from Egypt)																			
HS27	5.8	3.7	9.2	1.7	7.7	12.2	14.6	42.0	62.7	60.0	68.0	65.0	76.7	69.3	67.8	54.2	69.5	73.1	52.8
HS25	69.7	53.2	44.7	46.0	35.4	47.7	50.5	30.5	17.2	19.5	13.7	17.4	12.5	16.9	13.9	20.0	8.9	5.7	9.1
Percentage (%) share of major imports by USA from Egypt (in total imports from Egypt)																			
HS27	18.0	15.4	16.5	20.6	51.0	40.9	46.2	39.5	42.3	33.3	16.9	45.0	12.0	0.1	2.7	15.8	11.5	32.8	37.2
HS61	15.7	9.9	12.6	13.1	8.4	11.2	12.4	13.3	15.3	15.9	19.3	12.2	20.0	26.6	28.6	22.6	23.0	28.2	16.8
HS62	28.2	16.2	20.7	19.3	12.7	14.7	16.6	18.2	20.6	21.2	24.0	16.9	29.1	30.9	30.8	23.1	20.9	15.3	14.0
Percentage (%) share of major imports by China from South Africa (in total imports from South Africa)																			
HS26	35.8	42.3	24.5	34.3	41.4	41.1	33.1	57.6	60.4	65.2	67.4	66.3	66.9	64.7	58.0	58.4	66.3	68.7	73.4
HS72	19.4	19.6	31.1	25.3	18.2	15.9	20.8	14.1	17.4	11.5	9.5	7.1	9.1	13.2	18.1	18.6	10.3	8.9	9.6
HS74	4.2	5.9	4.7	1.7	2.7	3.3	2.5	2.8	1.9	1.9	1.8	2.0	2.0	1.9	2.8	2.3	2.5	3.9	3.5
HS51	3.8	2.2	1.1	1.4	1.5	2.1	1.6	1.9	2.2	1.0	1.0	1.9	1.8	2.4	2.8	3.2	3.3	3.4	1.9

	Period of years																		
	2001	2002	2003	2004	2005	2006	2007	2008	2009	2010	2011	2012	2013	2014	2015	2016	2017	2018	2019
Percentage (%) share of major imports by USA from South Africa (in total imports from South Africa)																			
HS71	39.4	5.7	32.5	33.1	34.9	40.3	46.1	31.9	22.3	28.1	25.3	20.0	22.9	20.0	26.3	23.6	25.9	30.9	34.9
HS72	7.9	11.6	8.4	15.5	10.8	10.9	9.7	13.5	6.6	10.3	9.6	10.5	9.8	14.4	8.4	10.5	11.8	10.0	7.6
HS87	10.0	18.5	15.4	11.4	6.2	9.8	9.0	23.4	33.8	28.1	28.4	28.8	24.6	18.7	19.5	21.0	17.3	6.8	7.1
HS84	7.7	10.0	5.5	5.3	7.0	6.2	5.8	5.5	5.3	5.2	5.8	6.4	6.6	8.2	9.2	9.0	6.2	6.9	6.5

Source: Own tables constructed using statistical data from the International Trade Centre trade database available at http://www.trademap.org.

Table A-10. Trade shares (%) of high value added products imported from the USA and China by Africa to Africa's total imports from these two countries

	Period of years																		
	2001	2002	2003	2004	2005	2006	2007	2008	2009	2010	2011	2012	2013	2014	2015	2016	2017	2018	2019
High skill- and technology-intensive manufactures imported by Africa from (Percentage (%) share to total imports by Africa from):																			
(i) the USA	25.7	25.0	21.7	22.1	24.4	20.3	17.9	19.2	19.8	17.8	15.7	17.7	17.0	19.9	22.6	22.6	21.0	21.8	22.7
(ii) China	16.9	16.9	15.3	14.5	15.2	14.4	13.8	13.4	14.3	13.2	14.4	14.0	14.2	15.1	15.0	15.3	16.5	17.2	16.0
Medium skill- and technology-intensive manufactures imported by Africa from (Percentage (%) share to total imports by Africa from):																			
(i) the USA	30.1	31.4	32.9	34.6	33.4	35.2	33.4	35.4	36.1	38.8	27.6	35.9	33.3	33.8	32.2	31.1	27.0	29.4	33.4
(ii) China	27.7	30.2	32.9	34.3	36.4	36.3	38.5	39.8	38.9	39.2	38.4	38.6	39.2	40.0	38.3	39.2	39.9	38.8	39.0

Table A-10. (Continued)

	Period of years																		
	2001	2002	2003	2004	2005	2006	2007	2008	2009	2010	2011	2012	2013	2014	2015	2016	2017	2018	2019
All high value added manufactures imported by Africa from (Percentage (%) share to total imports by Africa from):																			
(i) the USA	55.8	56.4	54.6	56.7	57.8	55.5	50.3	54.6	55.9	56.6	43.3	53.6	50.3	53.7	54.8	53.7	48.0	51.2	56.1
(ii) China	44.6	47.1	48.2	48.8	51.6	50.7	52.3	53.2	53.2	52.4	52.8	52.6	53.4	55.1	53.3	54.5	56.4	56.0	55.0

Source:Own tables constructed using statistical data from the International Trade Centre trade database available at http://www.trademap.org.

Notes: High skill- and technology-intensive manufactures are found in product categories HS28-HS39; HS85; HS90, HS91. Very few are found in product category HS84.

Medium skill- and technology-intensive manufactures are found in product categories HS40; HS84; HS87. Very few are found in product categories HS39 and HS85.

Harmonised system (HS) product classification by skill and technology intensity is provided by UNCTAD.

There are 19 broad product categories, at HS 2 digit level, which make up the High skill- and technology-intensive manufactures and the Medium skill- and technology-intensive manufactures. These are as follows:

HS28 (Inorganic chemicals; organic or inorganic compounds of precious metals, of rare-earth metals…); HS29 (Organic chemicals); HS30 (Pharmaceutical products); HS31 (Fertilisers); HS32 (Tanning or dyeing extracts; tannins and their derivatives; dyes, pigments and other colouring…); HS33 (Essential oils and resinoids; perfumery, cosmetic or toilet preparations); HS34 (Soap, organic surface-active agents, washing preparations, lubricating preparations, artificial ...); HS35 (Albuminoidal substances; modified starches; glues; enzymes; HS36 (Explosives; pyrotechnic products; matches; pyrophoric alloys; certain combustible preparations); HS37 (Photographic or cinematographic goods); HS38 (Miscellaneous chemical products); HS39 (Plastics and articles thereof); HS40 (Rubber and articles thereof); HS84 (Machinery, mechanical appliances, nuclear reactors, boilers; parts thereof); HS85 (Electrical machinery and equipment and parts thereof; sound recorders and reproducers, television); HS87 (Vehicles other than railway or tramway rolling stock, and parts and accessories thereof); HS88 (Aircraft, spacecraft, and parts thereof); HS90 (Optical, photographic, cinematographic, measuring, checking, precision, medical or surgical ...) HS91 (Clocks and watches and parts thereof).

Table A-11. Trade shares (%) of the specific high value added products imported from the USA and China by Africa to total imports from these two countries

	Period of years																		
	2001	2002	2003	2004	2005	2006	2007	2008	2009	2010	2011	2012	2013	2014	2015	2016	2017	2018	2019
Share of top 5 high value added manufactures imported by Africa from the USA (Percentage (%) of total imports from the USA)																			
HS84	19.7	20.7	22.3	23.5	22.6	23.8	20.5	22.6	22.6	23.5	14.8	20.0	22.4	20.5	20.3	19.6	17.9	15.1	15.4
HS87	3.9	4.1	4.4	5.8	5.8	6.8	8.1	7.1	8.9	11.3	10.9	13.7	10.2	9.3	8.3	8.2	8.5	8.4	11.4
HS85	7.4	7.7	7.5	6.9	7.1	6.6	6.7	8.0	7.4	6.9	4.8	6.5	5.8	6.5	7.6	6.5	6.8	5.1	5.0
HS88	12.5	10.2	8.0	6.8	10.5	5.8	4.4	5.8	4.9	2.9	4.9	2.9	2.1	7.2	7.0	7.7	5.3	8.2	9.4
HS90	4.0	4.5	4.0	4.6	4.5	4.1	3.9	4.0	4.3	4.3	2.8	3.9	4.1	3.8	4.3	4.6	4.3	3.8	3.8
Total of top 5	47.5	47.2	46.2	47.6	50.5	47.1	43.6	47.5	48.1	48.9	38.2	47.0	44.6	47.3	47.5	46.6	42.8	40.6	45.0
Share of top 5 high value added manufactures imported by Africa from China (Percentage (%) share of total imports from China)																			
HS85	14.3	15.2	15.8	17.8	18.2	17.6	17.5	18.7	18.9	19.5	18.4	16.2	16.6	18.8	19.9	19.8	19.9	19.9	19.3
HS84	12.2	13.8	15.3	14.7	15.9	16.0	17.2	18.4	17.6	17.3	17.5	18.2	18.4	18.4	16.9	18.3	18.6	17.5	18.1
HS87	3.2	4.0	5.7	6.4	7.3	8.2	9.7	9.0	8.0	8.5	7.0	8.7	8.2	7.4	6.4	5.3	5.6	5.3	5.7
HS39	2.3	2.5	2.1	2.0	2.3	2.5	2.7	2.5	2.6	2.3	2.7	2.8	3.6	3.2	3.1	3.2	3.4	3.9	3.7
HS40	2.4	2.1	2.1	2.1	2.3	1.9	2.1	1.9	2.1	2.1	2.6	2.7	2.8	2.5	2.1	2.3	2.4	2.3	2.2
Total of top 5	34.4	37.6	41.0	43.0	46.0	46.2	49.2	50.5	49.2	49.7	48.2	48.6	49.6	50.3	48.4	48.9	49.9	48.9	49.0

Source:Own tables constructed using statistical data from the International Trade Centre trade database available at http://www.trademap.org.

Notes: HS39 = Plastics and articles thereof; HS40 = Rubber and articles thereof; HS84 = Machinery, mechanical appliances, nuclear reactors, boilers; parts thereof; HS85 = Electrical machinery and equipment and parts thereof; sound recorders and reproducers, television; HS87 = Vehicles other than railway or tramway rolling stock, and parts and accessories thereof; HS88 = Aircraft, spacecraft, and parts thereof; HS90 = Optical, photographic, cinematographic, measuring, checking, precision, medical or surgical.

Table A-12. A comparison of Intra-Industry Trade (IIT) opportunities in China-Africa trade and USA- Africa trade (2001-2019)

	Period of years																		
	2001	2002	2003	2004	2005	2006	2007	2008	2009	2010	2011	2012	2013	2014	2015	2016	2017	2018	2019
Intra-Industry Trade (IIT) opportunities in China- Africa trade																			
HS31	0.676	0.204	0.356	0.318	0.768	0.703	0.523	0.866	0.850	0.855	0.003	0.508	0.148	0.209	0.068	0.012	0.152	0.032	0.166
Intra-Industry Trade (IIT) opportunities in USA- Africa trade																			
HS28	0.676	0.477	0.551	0.452	0.447	0.753	0.706	0.673	0.696	0.679	0.533	0.849	0.981	0.950	0.871	0.969	0.681	0.975	0.986
HS29	0.725	0.780	0.957	0.953	0.903	0.872	0.953	0.795	0.887	0.903	0.865	0.933	0.814	0.786	0.877	0.920	0.771	0.794	0.933
HS31	0.717	0.454	0.651	0.625	0.674	0.569	0.594	0.696	0.741	0.826	0.286	0.478	0.392	0.277	0.362	0.133	0.073	0.060	0.115
HS33	0.341	0.475	0.547	0.447	0.468	0.501	0.537	0.537	0.476	0.507	0.580	0.429	0.358	0.509	0.486	0.535	0.649	0.807	0.723
HS40	0.845	0.959	0.964	0.902	0.858	0.866	0.902	0.999	0.730	0.660	0.569	0.847	0.942	0.873	0.623	0.719	0.684	0.854	0.863
HS87	0.956	0.972	0.927	0.869	0.538	0.640	0.519	0.974	0.867	0.697	0.677	0.657	0.676	0.539	0.678	0.692	0.702	0.317	0.250
HS91	0.530	0.615	0.701	0.716	0.943	0.955	0.706	0.631	0.413	0.428	0.353	0.465	0.539	0.330	0.297	0.546	0.544	0.723	0.947

Source:Own tables constructed using statistical data from the International Trade Centre trade database available at http://www.trademap.org.

Table A-13. A comparison of Intra-Industry Trade (IIT) opportunities in China's trade and USA's trade with Algeria and Egypt (2001-2019)

	Period of years																		
	2001	2002	2003	2004	2005	2006	2007	2008	2009	2010	2011	2012	2013	2014	2015	2016	2017	2018	2019
Intra-Industry Trade (IIT) opportunities in USA- Algeria trade																			
HS28	0.000	0.013	0.001	0.795	0.856	0.050	0.908	0.010	0.000	0.000	0.001	0.002	0.020	0.010	0.788	0.753	0.000	..	..
HS29	0.486	0.932	0.011	0.000	0.584	0.879	0.220	0.827	0.157	0.010	0.000	0.000	0.001	0.874	0.445	0.242	0.000	..	..
Intra-Industry Trade (IIT) opportunities in China- Egypt trade																			
HS28	0.000	0.024	0.000	0.018	0.001	0.002	0.000	0.000	0.093	0.033	0.760	0.087	0.216	0.008	0.000	0.023	0.787	0.634	0.342
HS39	0.295	0.166	0.737	0.856	0.834	0.331	0.090	0.309	0.749	0.489	0.246	0.113	0.134	0.063	0.020	0.051	0.201	0.235	0.161
Intra-Industry Trade (IIT) opportunities in USA- Egypt trade																			
HS33	0.679	0.493	0.575	0.839	0.623	0.882	0.835	0.511	0.544	0.638	0.773	0.684	0.500	0.641	0.631	0.488	0.998	0.919	0.810

Source:Own tables constructed using statistical data from the International Trade Centre trade database available at http://www.trademap.org.

Notes: There are no intra-industry trade opportunities in the China-Algeria trade.

Table A-14. A comparison of Intra-Industry Trade (IIT) opportunities in China's trade and USA's trade with Angola and Nigeria (2001-2019)

	Period of years																		
	2001	2002	2003	2004	2005	2006	2007	2008	2009	2010	2011	2012	2013	2014	2015	2016	2017	2018	2019
Intra-Industry Trade (IIT) opportunities in China-Nigeria trade																			
HS38	0.708	0.981	0.697	n/a	n/a	0.753	0.974	0.021	0.862	0.951	0.920	0.904	0.873	0.954	0.978	1.000	0.969	0.952	0.973
Intra-Industry Trade (IIT) opportunities in USA-Nigeria trade																			
HS34	0.307	0.603	0.817	n/a	n/a	0.922	0.766	0.858	n/a	n/a	n/a	0.103	0.576	0.558	0.565	0.569	0.294	0.786	0.588

Source:Own tables constructed using statistical data from the International Trade Centre trade database available at http://www.trademap.org.

Notes: There are no intra-industry trade opportunities in both the China-Angola trade and the USA-Angola trade.

While there are intra-industry trade opportunities in trade with Nigeria, Nigeria's exports to China for most years were between US$1 000 and US$37 000 and exports to the USA for most years were between US$1 000 and US$200 000.

Table A-15. A comparison of Intra-Industry Trade (IIT) opportunities in China-South Africa trade and USA-South Africa trade (2001-2019)

	Period of years																		
	2001	2002	2003	2004	2005	2006	2007	2008	2009	2010	2011	2012	2013	2014	2015	2016	2017	2018	2019
Intra-Industry Trade (IIT) opportunities in China-South Africa trade																			
HS28	0.224	0.296	0.602	0.959	0.622	0.454	0.455	0.323	0.548	0.399	0.430	0.362	0.199	0.319	0.155	0.206	0.144	0.213	0.260
HS29	0.815	0.655	0.770	0.747	0.877	0.665	0.592	0.497	0.378	0.599	0.399	0.422	0.285	0.157	0.118	0.116	0.142	0.098	0.142
HS32	0.922	0.959	0.926	0.847	0.872	0.687	0.708	0.523	0.557	0.554	0.439	0.414	0.453	0.448	0.368	0.483	0.436	0.361	0.321
HS38	0.417	0.271	0.228	0.363	0.733	0.462	0.607	0.347	0.414	0.433	0.348	0.225	0.382	0.341	0.458	0.412	0.479	0.365	0.409
Intra-Industry Trade (IIT) opportunities in USA-South Africa trade																			
HS28	0.342	0.197	0.321	0.197	0.245	0.326	0.374	0.330	0.407	0.326	0.290	0.394	0.458	0.429	0.490	0.624	0.807	0.733	0.792
HS29	0.769	0.787	0.956	0.886	0.914	0.851	0.992	0.765	0.861	0.938	0.746	0.563	0.529	0.462	0.505	0.542	0.504	0.475	0.472
HS32	0.992	0.870	0.948	0.667	0.591	0.696	0.616	0.694	0.661	0.469	0.387	0.427	0.532	0.496	0.427	0.448	0.492	0.441	0.504
HS33	0.341	0.683	0.665	0.522	0.392	0.388	0.421	0.433	0.288	0.440	0.517	0.369	0.336	0.469	0.477	0.532	0.584	0.669	0.600
HS36	0.072	0.439	0.624	0.812	0.247	0.093	0.080	0.227	0.070	0.494	0.596	0.657	0.573	0.601	0.025	0.074	0.037	0.067	0.024
HS38	0.231	0.429	0.367	0.635	0.621	0.585	0.618	0.631	0.417	0.404	0.428	0.437	0.373	0.332	0.301	0.365	0.420	0.360	0.472
HS40	0.747	0.847	0.708	0.602	0.661	0.695	0.438	0.641	0.363	0.307	0.409	0.401	0.321	0.351	0.322	0.349	0.346	0.243	0.235
HS84	0.586	0.504	0.425	0.395	0.480	0.404	0.416	0.374	0.339	0.387	0.406	0.410	0.414	0.502	0.588	0.645	0.518	0.523	0.510
HS87	0.657	0.671	0.675	0.828	0.886	0.840	0.985	0.496	0.397	0.461	0.559	0.685	0.656	0.864	0.725	0.596	0.614	0.996	0.957

Source:Own tables constructed using statistical data from the International Trade Centre trade database available at http://www.trademap.org.

Table A-16. A comparison of exports of high value added manufactured goods to China and USA by Africa and South Africa (2001-2019)

Period of years																			
	2001	2002	2003	2004	2005	2006	2007	2008	2009	2010	2011	2012	2013	2014	2015	2016	2017	2018	2019
Africa's total exports of high value added manufactured goods (% share of Africa's total exports) to:																			
China	3.89	2.39	3.05	3.25	2.59	1.95	1.22	1.24	1.73	1.37	1.93	2.45	1.16	1.00	0.75	1.25	1.01	0.77	3.17
USA	5.84	7.47	5.71	4.59	3.48	3.41	3.39	4.20	6.29	6.20	7.36	7.99	11.30	14.45	20.39	15.72	13.83	13.91	15.01
South Africa's total exports of high value added manufactured goods (% share of South Africa's total exports) to:																			
China	20.94	11.15	15.35	18.65	14.62	9.76	6.20	6.73	4.41	4.73	2.77	4.78	4.37	4.06	2.57	2.72	2.60	2.45	2.90
USA	28.49	49.20	33.93	30.33	30.34	27.38	24.77	40.71	51.81	45.36	49.10	48.13	44.12	41.04	43.04	44.12	34.89	27.85	27.67

Source:Own tables constructed using statistical data from the International Trade Centre trade database available at http://www.trademap.org.

Notes: There are 19 broad product categories, at HS 2 digit level, which make up the High skill- and technology-intensive manufactures and the Medium skill- and technology-intensive manufactures. These are given in the notes under Table A-10 above.

Table A-17. Relative bilateral trade intensity between China and the selected African countries (2001-2019)

Period of years																			
	2001	2002	2003	2004	2005	2006	2007	2008	2009	2010	2011	2012	2013	2014	2015	2016	2017	2018	2019
Revealed trade preference index (RTP_{ij}) between Algeria and China																			
(RTP_{ij})	-0.36	-0.28	-0.24	-0.14	-0.15	-0.20	0.04	-0.02	0.20	0.07	0.06	0.13	0.14	0.18	0.29	0.36	0.31	..	..
Revealed trade preference index (RTP_{ij}) between Angola and China																			
(RTP_{ij})	..	..	..	0.98	1.00	1.00	0.85	..	0.85	0.90	0.87	0.93	0.92	0.93	0.90	0.91	0.97	0.98	..
Revealed trade preference index (RTP_{ij}) between Egypt and China																			
(RTP_{ij})	0.39	0.38	0.31	0.32	0.23	0.32	0.35	0.31	0.31	0.26	0.27	0.27	0.30	0.33	0.40	0.37	0.34	0.40	0.39
Revealed trade preference index (RTP_{ij}) between Nigeria and China																			
(RTP_{ij})	0.27	0.22	0.18	..	..	0.03	0.22	0.17	0.31	0.14	0.10	0.19	0.28	0.34	0.49	0.46	0.50	0.45	0.56
Revealed trade preference index (RTP_{ij}) between South Africa and China																			
(RTP_{ij})	0.29	0.32	0.33	0.34	0.36	0.40	0.46	0.48	0.56	0.55	0.65	0.72	0.76	0.72	0.68	0.63	0.63	0.62	0.64

Source: Own tables constructed using statistical data from the International Trade Centre trade database available at http://www.trademap.org.

Table A-18. Relative bilateral trade intensity between the United States of America and the selected African countries (20101-2019)

Period of years																			
	2001	2002	2003	2004	2005	2006	2007	2008	2009	2010	2011	2012	2013	2014	2015	2016	2017	2018	2019
Revealed trade preference index (RTP_{ij}) between Algeria and United States of America																			
(RTP_{ij})	0.32	0.29	0.46	0.57	0.60	0.700	0.74	0.65	0.55	0.61	0.55	0.35	0.08	0.10	0.02	0.16	0.07	..	..
Revealed trade preference index (RTP_{ij}) between Angola and United States of America																			
(RTP_{ij})	..	..	..	1.00	1.00	1.00	0.75	..	0.60	0.65	0.69	0.38	0.31	0.17	0.02	0.24	-.0.00	-0.07	..
Revealed trade preference index (RTP_{ij}) between Egypt and United States of America																			
(RTP_{ij})	0.57	0.55	0.52	0.52	0.43	0.47	0.47	0.34	0.35	0.35	0.31	0.24	0.17	0.17	0.04	-0.05	0.03	0.11	0.16
Revealed trade preference index (RTP_{ij}) between Nigeria and United States of America																			
(RTP_{ij})	0.85	0.73	0.82	..	..	0.91	0.93	0.92	0.76	0.83	0.73	0.57	0.43	0.10	0.03	0.28	0.44	0.22	0.18
Revealed trade preference index (RTP_{ij}) between South Africa and United States of America																			
(RTP_{ij})	0.36	0.32	0.31	0.28	0.23	0.27	0.31	0.34	0.27	0.24	0.24	022	0.20	0.17	0.15	0.13	0.15	0.13	0.14

Source: Own tables constructed using statistical data from the International Trade Centre trade database available at http://www.trademap.org.

Table A-19. A comparison of China's relative bilateral trade intensity with various regional groups (2001-2019)

Period of years																			
	2001	2002	2003	2004	2005	2006	2007	2008	2009	2010	2011	2012	2013	2014	2015	2016	2017	2018	2019
Revealed trade preference index (RTP_{ij}) between Africa and China																			
(RTP_{ij})	0.36	0.34	0.37	0.46	0.48	0.47	0.48	0.55	0.52	0.51	0.51	0.55	0.57	0.58	0.57	0.55	0.57	0.59	0.62
Revealed trade preference index (RTP_{ij}) between America and China																			
(RTP_{ij})	0.31	0.35	0.39	0.41	0.40	0.41	0.42	0.42	0.46	0.46	0.46	0.44	0.44	0.42	0.41	0.42	0.46	0.47	0.41
Revealed trade preference index (RTP_{ij}) between Europe and China																			
(RTP_{ij})	-0.19	-0.23	-0.24	-0.25	-0.22	-0.21	-0.20	-0.17	-0.16	-0.12	-0.12	-0.14	-0.17	-0.14	-0.14	-0.13	-0.12	-0.12	-0.10
Revealed trade preference index (RTP_{ij}) between OPEC and China																			
(RTP_{ij})	0.28	0.27	0.28	0.30	0.22	0.31	0.30	0.31	0.47	0.45	0.52	0.37	0.36	0.38	0.38	0.40	0.43	0.44	0.53

Source: Own tables constructed using statistical data from the International Trade Centre trade database available at http://www.trademap.org.

Table A-20. A comparison of the United States of America's relative bilateral trade intensity with various regional groups (2001-2019)

Period of years																			
	2001	2002	2003	2004	2005	2006	2007	2008	2009	2010	2011	2012	2013	2014	2015	2016	2017	2018	2019
Revealed trade preference index (RTP_{ij}) between Africa and United States of America																			
(RTP_{ij})	0.42	0.37	0.45	0.56	0.62	0.58	0.55	0.59	0.40	0.44	0.42	0.24	0.15	0.05	-0.04	-0.00	0.02	-0.01	-0.03
Revealed trade preference index (RTP_{ij}) between Asia and the United States of America																			
(RTP_{ij})	0.57	0.57	0.54	0.52	0.48	0.50	0.46	0.42	0.45	0.42	0.39	0.35	0.36	0.36	0.38	0.41	0.39	0.39	0.36
Revealed trade preference index (RTP_{ij}) between Europe and the United States of America																			
(RTP_{ij})	0.17	0.14	0.11	0.09	0.11	0.11	0.10	0.13	0.18	0.21	0.22	0.26	0.26	0.26	0.30	0.28	0.28	0.28	0.31
Revealed trade preference index (RTP_{ij}) between OPEC and the United States of America																			
(RTP_{ij})	0.61	0.56	0.57	0.64	0.54	0.66	0.50	0.53	0.49	0.52	0.55	0.32	0.26	0.21	0.12	0.17	0.14	0.11	0.01

Source: Own tables constructed using statistical data from the International Trade Centre trade database available at http://www.trademap.org.

Table A-21. Revealed Trade Barriers ((RTB^j_{ik}) indexes for Africa's top 20 products exported to China

Period of years																			
	2001	2002	2003	2004	2005	2006	2007	2008	2009	2010	2011	2012	2013	2014	2015	2016	2017	2018	2019
Revealed Trade Barriers ((RTB^j_{ik}) indexes for Africa's top 20 products exported to China																			
HS27	7,31	7,23	7,11	6,00	5,20	4,83	5,78	4,6	5,04	4,43	3,76	3,95	3,94	4,37	5,78	5,99	5,48	4,86	4,97
HS26	12,2	13,6	8,54	12,4	9,92	10,6	6,45	7,37	11,2	9,89	10,5	8,70	11,5	9,76	12,4	16.0	14,3	13,2	13,7
HS74	1,30	1,66	1,53	1,07	3,35	1,52	1,07	1,82	2,90	5,00	4,74	5,26	5,13	5,18	6,48	8,67	5,36	5,83	8,10
HS81	3,22	3,04	3,93	3,91	2,18	3,32	2,33	4,69	6,31	9,30	6,09	5,99	8,31	8,56	16,2	22,7	32,1	36,7	24,7
HS44	5,97	6,37	4,09	3,68	3,61	3,00	1,88	1,75	1,8	1,86	1,28	1,37	1,39	1,79	2,19	2,92	2,47	2,53	2,64
HS12	0,03	0,08	0,27	0,66	1,79	0,98	0,71	0,40	1,30	1,08	1,11	1,05	1,47	2,80	2,88	3,48	1,99	1,51	3,46
HS72	1,26	1,29	1,95	1,23	0,74	0,71	0,87	0,37	1,06	0,69	0,70	0,40	0,70	0,80	1,35	1,88	0,79	0,49	0,67
HS52	0,36	2,28	6,04	7,82	7,79	8,23	2,05	1,15	2,06	1,33	1,64	2,97	2,82	1,31	1,26	1,39	0,96	1,37	1,44
HS51	2,65	1,51	1,07	1,21	1,45	2,59	2,17	2,04	4,00	2,02	2,32	3,31	4,01	4,39	5,66	8,23	7,79	5,92	4,57
HS25	2,09	2,93	1,34	2,24	1,28	1,25	0,67	0,54	0,64	0,49	0,64	0,42	0,47	0,38	0,48	0,73	0,70	0,66	0,93
HS03	0,77	0,84	0,84	0,58	0,44	0,25	0,13	0,08	0,09	0,14	0,21	0,28	0,29	0,27	0,39	0,73	0,43	0,34	0,41
HS18	0,95	1,11	0,5	0,88	1,38	1,23	0,78	0,79	0,38	0,23	0,55	0,74	0,47	0,63	0,52	0,52	0,38	0,38	0,90
HS71	0,01	0,02	0,09	0,09	0,17	1,48	0,16	0,30	0,40	0,24	0,17	0,13	0,15	0,13	0,18	0,20	0,07	0,12	0,07
HS47	7,21	6,48	1,77	4,50	0,23	0,20	0,36	0,61	1,04	0,54	0,84	0,77	1,08	1,88	2,15	2,57	1,58	1,11	0,71
HS39	0,05	0,03	0,06	0,08	0,11	0,07	0,06	0,10	0,15	0,09	0,08	0,06	0,07	0,07	0,05	0,07	0,07	0,06	0,06
HS75	0,34	0,69	1,79	0,70	2,74	1,44	0,43	0,64	1,26	1,37	0,98	0,81	1,27	0,96	2,35	4,79	2,72	0,89	1,00
HS41	0,73	0,69	0,38	1,15	1,43	0,86	1,37	1,06	1,44	7,25	1,32	1,87	1,55	1,47	1,99	2,22	1,96	1,30	1,31
HS84	0,11	0,02	0,04	0,05	0,03	0,02	0,02	0,01	0,01	0,01	0,01	0,01	0,02	0,02	0,01	0,01	0,01	0,01	0,01

Table A-21. (Continued)

Period of years																			
	2001	2002	2003	2004	2005	2006	2007	2008	2009	2010	2011	2012	2013	2014	2015	2016	2017	2018	2019
HS24	0,56	0,59	2,80	7,21	2,80	1,36	1,06	0,43	0,70	1,65	1,25	0,48	0,68	0,76	0,53	0,71	0,53	0,61	0,24
HS29	0,21	0,18	0,20	0,24	0,20	0,15	0,09	0,07	0,05	0,10	0,05	0,05	0,03	0,02	0,02	0,04	0,04	0,02	0,03

Source: Own tables constructed using statistical data from the International Trade Centre trade database available at http://www.trademap.org.

Notes: HS 27 = Mineral fuels, mineral oils and products of their distillation...; HS26 = Ores, slag and ash; HS74 = Copper and articles thereof; HS81 = Other base metals; cements; articles thereof; HS44= Wood and articles of wood; wood charcoal; HS12= Oil seeds and oleaginous fruits; miscellaneous grains …; HS72 = Iron and steel; HS52 = Cotton; HS51 = Wool, fine or coarse animal hair; horsehair yarn and woven fabric; HS25 = Salt; sulphur; earths ...; HS03 = Fish and crustaceans, molluscs and other aquatic invertebrates; HS18 = Cocoa and cocoa preparations; HS71 = Natural or cultured pearls, precious…; HS47 = Pulp of wood or of other fibrous cellulosic material; recovered (waste & scrap) paper or….; HS39 = Plastics and articles thereof; HS75 = Nickel and articles thereof; HS41 = Raw hides and skins (other than fur skins) and leather; HS84 = Machinery, mechanical appliances, nuclear reactors… ; HS24 = Tobacco and manufactured tobacco substitutes; HS29 = Organic chemicals.

Table A-22. Revealed Trade Barriers ((RTB^j_{ik}) indexes for Africa's top 20 products exported to the United States of America

Period of years																			
	2001	2002	2003	2004	2005	2006	2007	2008	2009	2010	2011	2012	2013	2014	2015	2016	2017	2018	2019
Revealed Trade Barriers ((RTB^j_{ik}) index for Africa's top 20 products exported to China																			
HS27	7,36	7,85	7,28	6,88	6.08	5.75	6.02	4.91	5.53	5.22	4.55	4.14	3.72	3.23	2.98	4.92	4.26	3.56	3.26
HS71	3,40	0,67	2,38	2,20	1.90	2.03	2.47	1.23	1.00	1.15	0.85	0.74	1.22	1.77	2.82	1.87	2.23	2.99	3.02
HS62	1,46	1,97	2,13	1,35	0.85	0.71	0.56	0.53	1.32	0.92	1.03	1.23	2.00	3.01	3.99	3.55	3.33	3.58	4.69
HS26	2,68	2,12	1,65	0,85	0.44	0.62	0.64	0.61	1.04	0.66	0.57	0.96	1.80	2.44	2.66	2.14	1.86	2.02	2.71
HS61	1,11	1,17	1,23	1,69	1,04	0,78	0,41	0,48	0,99	0,63	0,70	0,99	1,24	2,13	2,39	2,09	2,33	2,46	3,39
HS18	5,80	8,09	5,06	5,55	5,82	4,06	2,97	2,84	5,95	4,28	5,52	8,63	11,2	15,4	20,3	15,5	15,9	12,7	14,1

Period of years																			
	2001	2002	2003	2004	2005	2006	2007	2008	2009	2010	2011	2012	2013	2014	2015	2016	2017	2018	2019
HS72	0,73	0,92	0,59	0,79	0,40	0,47	0,32	0,31	0,27	0,39	0,35	0,55	0,83	1,53	1,23	1,34	1,59	1,26	1,20
HS84	0,10	0,10	0,07	0,06	0,05	0,05	0,05	0,04	0,06	0,06	0,06	0,09	0,16	0,24	0,33	0,24	0,17	0,19	0,20
HS09	2,85	3,40	3,15	2,02	0,89	0,63	0,85	0,62	1,07	0,92	0,86	1,18	2,28	3,63	5,48	5,56	8,17	7,76	8,76
HS87	0,19	0,25	0,22	0,16	0,07	0,11	0,11	0,24	0,48	0,38	0,39	0,50	0,62	0,59	0,76	0,60	0,54	0,21	0,25
HS76	0,40	0,55	0,41	0,48	0,66	0,54	0,42	0,20	0,53	0,48	0,35	0,53	0,74	1,05	0,86	1,22	1,50	2,31	1,96
HS08	0,31	0,41	0,32	0,28	0,26	0,25	0,20	0,17	0,26	0,35	0,31	0,46	0,94	1,23	1,90	1,31	1,43	2,04	2,26
HS29	0,23	0,32	0.,29	0,22	0,25	0,17	0,24	0,24	0,23	0,28	0,24	0,30	0,47	0,77	0,77	0,58	0,63	0,59	0,69
HS85	0,01	0,01	0,01	0,01	0,01	0,01	0,01	0,01	0,02	0,02	0,02	0,03	0,05	0,06	0,09	0,08	0,06	0,07	0,08
HS40	0,31	0,39	0,30	0,33	0,25	0,27	0,23	0,23	0,27	0,35	1,24	0,62	0,95	0,77	0,58	0,59	0,47	0,69	0,77
HS28	1,00	1,87	0,98	0,99	0,96	0,45	0,43	0,36	0,53	0,59	0,67	0,53	0,74	1,10	1,55	0,96	0,80	1,20	1,50
HS25	1,66	1,73	1,23	1,05	0,82	0,68	0,67	1,14	1,37	1,27	1,54	2,27	3,42	2,49	2,26	1,44	2,04	2,00	2,12
HS57	0,30	0,29	0,19	0,12	0,10	0,12	0,15	0,71	2,28	1,97	1,91	2,64	4,97	6,73	7,97	7,18	6,07	6,44	7,86
HS15	0,14	0,07	0,06	0,36	0,25	0,31	0,26	0,21	0,40	0,28	0,27	0,32	0,58	0,57	2,04	1,11	0,67	1,40	1,19
HS03	0,31	0,38	0,32	0,24	0,17	0,14	0,15	0,10	0,11	0,27	0,10	0,14	0,30	0,37	1,21	1,02	0,66	0,56	0,62

Source: Own tables constructed using statistical data from the International Trade Centre trade database available at http://www.trademap.org.

Notes:

HS27 = Mineral fuels, mineral oils and products of their distillation; mineral …..; HS71 = Natural or cultured pearls, precious or semi-precious stones…..; HS62 = Articles of apparel and clothing accessories… ; HS26 = Ores, slag and ash; HS61 = Articles of apparel and clothing accessories, knitted or crocheted….; HS18 = Cocoa and cocoa preparations; HS72 = Iron and steelHS84 = Machinery, mechanical appliances, nuclear reactors…..HS09 = Coffee, tea, maté and spices; HS87 = Vehicles other than railway or tramway rolling stock….HS76 = Aluminium and articles thereof; HS08 = Edible fruit & nuts; peel of citrus fruit...; HS29 = Organic chemicals; HS85 = Electrical machinery & equipment and parts thereof…..; HS40 = Rubber and articles thereof; HS28 = Inorganic chemicals; organic or inorganic compounds of precious metals…; HS25 = Salt; sulphur; earths and stone…..; HS57 = Carpets & other textile floor coverings; HS15 = Animal or vegetable fats and oils and their cleavage products; prepared edible fats….; HS03 = Fish and crustaceans, molluscs and other aquatic invertebrates…

Table A-23. China-Africa trade complementarity from Africa's perspective (2001-2019)

Period of years																			
	2001	2002	2003	2004	2005	2006	2007	2008	2009	2010	2011	2012	2013	2014	2015	2016	2017	2018	2019
Trade complementarity in Food, basic (SITC 0 + 22 + 4) with																			
China	99.50	99.63	99.57	99.74	99.81	99.70	99.42	99.02	99.11	99.24	99.06	99.32	99.33	99.15	99.46	99.45	99.45	99.41	99.60
Trade complementarity in Beverages and tobacco (SITC 1)with																			
China	99.05	99.21	98.83	98.71	99.04	99.30	99.62	99.08	98.63	99.15	99.11	99.18	98.74	99.23	99.47	99.71	99.08	99.38	99.31
Trade complementarity in Agricultural raw materials (SITC 2 less 22, 27 and 28) with																			
China	99.89	99.91	99.98	99.60	99.85	99.70	99.73	99.81	99.76	99.53	99.07	99.08	98.89	98.90	99.04	98.41	98.12	97.91	97.37
Trade complementarity in Non-ferrous metals (SITC 68) with																			
China	98.71	98.92	98.67	98.47	97.86	97.02	96.39	95.98	96.79	95.91	95.80	94.89	94.50	94.59	93.97	94.25	94.72	94.86	94.53
Trade complementarity in Other ores and metals (SITC 27 + 28) with																			
China	99.97	99.97	99.97	99.93	99.70	99.82	99.79	99.91	99.83	99.99	99.83	99.80	99.90	99.94	99.98	99.83	99.94	98.99	99.98
Trade complementarity in Fuels (SITC 3) with																			
China	99.64	99.83	99.82	99.93	99.86	99.81	99.75	99.41	99.38	99.17	98.90	98.91	98.99	98.79	99.15	99.12	99.23	98.99	98.50
Trade complementarity in Chemical products (SITC 5) with																			
China	99.84	99.89	99.95	99.79	99.27	99.08	98.93	98.62	98.69	98.49	98.15	98.03	97.90	97.42	97.29	97.40	96.98	96.43	96.48
Trade complementarity in Machinery and transport equipment (SITC 7) with																			
China	99.05	98.57	97.92	97.44	96.56	95.90	95.07	94.43	94.30	93.56	93.23	92.67	92.15	91.26	90.46	90.38	89.61	89.17	89.11
Trade complementarity in Other manufactured goods (SITC 6 + 8 less 667 and 68) with																			
China	97.30	97.06	96.28	95.48	94.15	93.01	92.76	92.32	92.07	91.19	90.44	89.19	88.76	87.28	86.59	86.42	86.28	86.13	86.36
Trade complementarity in Iron and Steel (SITC 67) with																			
China	99.70	99.65	99.34	99.42	98.87	97.89	96.52	95.27	97.86	96.19	96.11	95.83	95.46	93.61	92.40	90.56	91.81	91.37	90.76
Trade complementarity in Textile fibres, yarn, fabrics and clothing (SITC 26 + 65 + 84) with																			
China	96.19	95.80	94.14	92.87	90.48	88.94	89.04	88.94	87.13	86.69	86.07	83.99	83.15	81.94	81.82	81.58	81.28	81.11	81.02

Source: Own tables constructed using imports and exports trade statistical data from UNCTAD available at https://unctadstat.unctad.org/wds/ReportFolders/reportFolders.aspx.

Table A-24. USA-Africa trade complementarity from Africa's perspective (2001-2019)

Period of years																			
	2001	2002	2003	2004	2005	2006	2007	2008	2009	2010	2011	2012	2013	2014	2015	2016	2017	2018	2019
Trade complementarity in Food, basic (SITC 0 + 22 + 4) with																			
USA	95.93	96.46	96.24	96.54	96.52	96.72	96.29	97.51	98.13	97.87	98.10	98.21	98.29	98.35	98.34	98.75	98.78	98.65	98.72
Trade complementarity in Beverages and tobacco (SITC 1)with																			
USA	97.63	98.71	98.95	98.99	99.07	98.97	99.29	99.41	99.63	99.65	99.77	99.74	99.69	99.69	99.70	99.86	99.66	99.91	99.99
Trade complementarity in Agricultural raw materials (SITC 2 less 22, 27 and 28) with																			
USA	97.19	97.69	97.82	97.91	97.57	98.04	97.99	97.67	97.67	97.22	96.93	96.73	96.89	96.86	96.85	96.91	96.72	97.11	97.29
Trade complementarity in Non-ferrous metals (SITC 68) with																			
USA	98.90	99.11	99.39	99.32	99.25	99.22	99.35	99.46	99.66	99.55	99.57	99.65	99.68	99.83	99.70	99.60	99.77	99.87	99.96
Trade complementarity in Other ores and metals (SITC 27 + 28) with																			
USA	98.73	97.99	98.33	98.24	98.19	97.86	97.45	97.57	98.49	98.38	98.20	98.52	98.00	97.65	98.76	99.01	99.29	98.84	98.94
Trade complementarity in Fuels (SITC 3) with																			
USA	99.97	99.85	99.90	99.94	99.93	99.59	99.56	99.99	99.85	99.89	98.62	99.63	99.48	99.47	99.17	99.46	98.83	98.72	98.61
Trade complementarity in Chemical products (SITC 5) with																			
USA	96.90	97.03	97.26	97.28	97.31	97.27	97.21	97.58	97.44	97.31	97.62	97.50	97.86	97.93	97.73	98.05	98.15	98.21	98.11
Trade complementarity in Machinery and transport equipment (SITC 7) with																			
USA	94.17	94.82	95.78	96.30	96.13	96.13	96.45	96.58	97.03	96.88	96.90	96.88	97.11	97.11	96.72	96.87	97.28	97.58	97.24
Trade complementarity in Other manufactured goods (SITC 6 + 8 less 667 and 68) with																			
USA	97.86	97.86	98.41	98.40	98.35	98.41	98.45	98.60	98.51	98.48	98.67	98.74	98.85	98.99	98.91	98.99	99.01	99.25	99.15
Trade complementarity in Iron and Steel (SITC 67) with																			
USA	99.16	98.82	99.15	99.25	98.91	99.30	99.05	99.48	99.71	99.53	99.53	99.45	99.66	99.64	99.60	99.64	99.60	99.99	99.83
Trade complementarity in Textile fibres, yarn, fabrics and clothing (SITC 26 + 65 + 84) with																			
USA	99.42	99.54	99.61	99.69	99.68	99.73	99.86	99.85	99.80	99.62	99.76	99.88	99.95	99.99	99.99	99.94	99.95	99.95	99.91

Source: Own tables constructed using imports and exports trade statistical data from UNCTAD available at https://unctadstat.unctad.org/wds/ReportFolders/reportFolders.aspx.

Table A-25. Percentage shares of SITC product categories in China-Africa import trade to Africa's total imports

Period of years																			
	2001	2002	2003	2004	2005	2006	2007	2008	2009	2010	2011	2012	2013	2014	2015	2016	2017	2018	2019
Percentage (%) share of Africa's world imports of Food, basic (SITC 0 + 22 + 4) with																			
China	1.87	1.90	2.31	1.79	2.01	2.32	2.06	2.04	2.41	2.29	2.43	2.86	3.08	2.59	3.11	2.85	3.17	3.34	3.62
Percentage (%) share of Africa's world imports of Beverages and tobacco (SITC 1)with																			
China	1.21	1.13	1.86	2.13	1.65	1.61	1.47	1.20	1.38	1.44	1.46	1.17	1.36	1.37	1.17	0.80	1.23	0.95	1.04
Percentage (%) share of Africa's world imports of Agricultural raw materials (SITC 2 less 22, 27 and 28) with																			
China	0.79	0.93	1.10	1.74	1.91	1.98	2.46	2.65	2.53	2.90	3.72	3.78	4.45	5.12	6.00	6.84	8.23	8.47	9.43
Percentage (%) share of Africa's world imports of Non-ferrous metals (SITC 68) with																			
China	3.38	2.87	3.51	4.07	5.47	7.49	9.74	11.38	10.61	12.41	12.96	15.33	16.46	15.86	17.49	16.76	15.76	15.49	16.30
Percentage (%) share of Africa's world imports of Other ores and metals (SITC 27 + 28) with																			
China	1.25	1.45	1.45	1.66	1.41	1.18	1.16	0.88	1.93	1.84	1.43	1.36	1.17	1.49	1.65	1.77	1.44	1.43	1.83
Percentage (%) share of Africa's world imports of Fuels (SITC 3) with																			
China	0.62	0.48	0.63	0.54	0.40	0.37	0.32	0.38	0.27	0.27	0.27	01.7	0.28	0.36	0.50	0.87	0.98	0.95	0.69
Percentage (%) share of Africa's world imports of Chemical products (SITC 5) with																			
China	2.69	2.87	2.98	3.31	4.51	5.11	5.55	6.47	6.96	6.93	7.82	8.42	9.06	10.19	10.41	10.00	10.89	12.15	12.11
Percentage (%) share of Africa's world imports of Machinery and transport equipment (SITC 7) with																			
China	3.64	4.45	5.83	6.74	8.72	10.36	12.32	14.36	14.71	16.10	16.70	17.76	18.85	20.87	22.49	22.48	23.74	24.64	25.08
Percentage (%) share of Africa's world imports of Other manufactured goods (SITC 6 + 8 less 667 and 68) with																			
China	7.92	8.34	10.36	12.13	14.83	17.43	18.31	19.49	20.73	22.26	23.80	27.04	27.84	31.24	33.19	32.93	33.06	33.46	33.19
Percentage (%) share of Africa's world imports of Iron and Steel (SITC 67) with																			
China	1.45	1.62	2.86	3.86	4.43	7.00	10.20	14.30	14.33	13.15	12.89	14.05	16.39	19.73	23.58	26.82	23.75	25.74	26.30
Percentage (%) share of Africa's world imports of Textile fibres, yarn, fabrics and clothing (SITC 26 + 65 + 84) with																			
China	10.62	11.35	15.43	18.43	23.20	26.71	27.14	26.98	30.96	31.85	33.29	38.09	39.49	42.55	43.48	43.37	44.06	44.40	44.75

Source: Own tables constructed using imports and exports trade statistical data from UNCTAD available at https://unctadstat.unctad.org/wds/ReportFolders/reportFolders.aspx.

Table A-26. Percentage shares of SITC product categories in USA-Africa import trade to Africa's total imports

Period of years																			
	2001	2002	2003	2004	2005	2006	2007	2008	2009	2010	2011	2012	2013	2014	2015	2016	2017	2018	2019
Percentage (%) share of Africa's world imports of Food, basic (SITC 0 + 22 + 4) with																			
USA	12.36	11.70	12.05	12.14	11.64	11.23	13.61	10.30	8.15	9.43	9.26	7.76	7.24	6.62	6.00	5.03	5.04	6.05	5.77
Percentage (%) share of Africa's world imports of Beverages and tobacco (SITC 1)with																			
USA	5.36	3.11	2.68	3.17	3.08	3.20	2.66	2.19	1.92	1.80	1.29	1.66	1.48	1.75	1.56	0.87	1.24	1.23	1.19
Percentage (%) share of Africa's world imports of Agricultural raw materials (SITC 2 less 22, 27 and 28) with																			
USA	6.92	5.69	5.40	5.26	5.96	4.96	5.31	6.27	6.37	7.34	7.90	8.50	8.23	8.36	8.30	7.87	8.29	7.71	7.29
Percentage (%) share of Africa's world imports of Non-ferrous metals (SITC 68) with																			
China	3.38	2.87	3.51	4.07	5.47	7.49	9.74	11.38	10.61	12.41	12.96	15.33	16.46	15.86	17.49	16.76	15.76	15.49	16.30
USA	2.48	2.17	1.57	1.63	1.84	1.79	1.81	1.39	1.06	1.30	1.32	1.13	0.93	0.86	0.80	0.98	0.69	0.72	0.53
Percentage (%) share of Africa's world imports of Other ores and metals (SITC 27 + 28) with																			
USA	3.28	4.47	3.86	4.31	4.45	5.27	5.97	6.46	3.80	4.22	5.04	4.00	5.98	6.69	3.77	2.75	2.60	3.87	3.13
Percentage (%) share of Africa's world imports of Fuels (SITC 3) with																			
USA	1.72	1.61	1.54	1.38	1.31	1.29	1.98	2.97	3.30	3.38	5.46	3.10	4.99	5.20	4.18	2.93	4.55	4.54	4.46
Percentage (%) share of Africa's world imports of Chemical products (SITC 5) with																			
USA	7.31	7.01	6.42	6.43	6.31	6.54	6.80	6.02	6.41	6.59	6.04	6.37	5.66	5.50	5.83	5.06	4.87	4.74	5.10
Percentage (%) share of Africa's world imports of Machinery and transport equipment (SITC 7) with																			
USA	13.45	11.84	9.86	8.90	9.43	9.73	9.17	9.25	8.57	8.40	8.36	8.61	8.20	8.31	8.54	7.79	6.76	6.24	7.04
Percentage (%) share of Africa's world imports of Other manufactured goods (SITC 6 + 8 less 667 and 68) with																			
USA	5.29	5.35	4.18	4.33	4.50	4.46	4.40	4.09	4.54	4.52	4.01	3.83	3.58	3.36	3.37	3.02	2.89	2.50	2.71
Percentage (%) share of Africa's world imports of Iron and Steel (SITC 67) with																			
USA	3.84	5.09	3.74	2.91	4.30	4.01	4.26	3.01	4.30	2.65	2.89	3.12	2.81	2.97	2.89	1.86	2.13	1.05	1.26
Percentage (%) share of Africa's world imports of Textile fibres, yarn, fabrics and clothing (SITC 26 + 65 + 84) with																			
USA	1.16	0.93	0.77	0.62	0.65	0.55	0.28	0.30	0.40	0.76	0.48	0.23	0.10	0.03	0.01	0.12	0.09	0.10	0.17

Source: Own tables constructed using imports and exports trade statistical data from UNCTAD available at https://unctadstat.unctad.org/wds/ReportFolders/reportFolders.aspx.

In: US-China Trade
Editor: John C. Amon
ISBN: 978-1-53619-956-7

Chapter 2

THE HISTORY OF SINO-US TRADE

***Jiandong Shi*[*]**
Doctoral School of Public Administration Sciences,
University of Public Service, Budapest, Hungary

ABSTRACT

This research analyzes the overall situation of the development of the Sino-US trade. First, the evolution process of Sino-US trade relations is sorted out and divided into four stages: Sino-US trade review from the Qing Dynasty to the Second World War; Sino-US trade review from the Second World War to the establishment of the People's Republic of China; Sino-US trade review from the establishment of the People's Republic of China to the establishment of Sino-US diplomatic relations; the development and change of Sino-US trade after the establishment of Sino-US diplomatic relations. Second, from the perspective of total trade volume, China's trade surplus with the U.S has been constantly increasing, which indicates that Chinese exports are increasingly dependent on the American market, and aggravates the asymmetry of Sino-US trade relations. The asymmetry of Sino-US trade relations has also brought great uncertainty and risk to the development of China's economy and foreign trade.

---

[*] Corresponding Author's E-mail: shijiandong1101@qq.com.

Finally, the trade imbalance between China and the U.S. is the major obstacle to the development of Sino-U.S. trade relations as well as the direct cause of Sino-US trade war.

Keywords: Sino-US trade, history, imbalance, friction

INTRODUCTION

The exchanges between China and the U.S. started from the trade in the late 18th century. The Qing government of China (1644-1912) and the American government officially recognized each other in 1844 (Liu, 2019). Sino-US trade relations have gone through four periods. Sino-US trade from the Qing Dynasty to the Second World War; Sino-US trade from the Second World War to the establishment of the People's Republic of China; Sino-US trade from the establishment of the People's Republic of China to the establishment of Sino-US diplomatic relations; Sino-US trade after the establishment of Sino-US diplomatic relations.

THE SINO-US TRADE FROM THE QING DYNASTY TO THE SECOND WORLD WAR

The first stage is the informal or non-treaty contact period from 1784 to 1844. The development of American shipping promoted the trade with China during this period. The Empress of China arrived in Guangzhou in 1784 ushered in a new era of Sino-US trade. The United States Congress formulated the early customs duty clauses to encourage direct US import from China. After the outbreak of the French Revolution, the European wars accelerated the development of Sino-US trade. The U.S. re-exported the imported Chinese tea to Europe and thus expanded the Chinese tea market.

American furs, sandalwood and other products sold well in Chinese market, which promoted the leaping development of the trade between the two countries. The end of the war between Britain and the U.S. in 1812 stimulated the U.S. trade with China. Cotton, opium, tea and silk were the main traded goods during this period (Pan, 2013). At that time, since China adopted an attitude of rejecting foreign objects, it was unable to accept a large number of foreign products and naturally had little demand for American products, which led to China's long-term trade surplus with the U.S. at that time. In order to compensate for this trade balance, the U.S. first sold British cotton cloth and eventually even smuggled opium to China.

In 1805 or earlier, the American merchants transported opium from Turkey for sale. In that year, the American merchants transported 124 bags and 51 boxes of opium, and exported 102 boxes of them to China in 1806, 180 boxes in 1807 and 1,741 boxes in 1829 (Liu, 2010). The import of opium caused the outflow of a large amount of silver from China, led to the decline of China's purchasing power and affected the export of American manufactured goods to China. In 1839, the value of American exports to China was $1.53 million, and that of Chinese exports to the U.S. was $3.68 million. The China and Britain Opium War broke out in 1840, and the Qing government signed the Treaty of Nanjing with Britain on August 29, 1842, which endowed Britain with a lot of privileges. Affected by Britain, the U.S. and the Qing government signed the Treaty of Wangxia on July 3, 1844, which marked the start of unequal Sino-US trade and the end of early Sino-US trade relations (Liang, 1985).

The second stage is the period of temporary expansion and continuous decline from 1845 to 1894. Affected by Taiping Heavenly Kingdom Movement, China's national purchasing power was reduced. Meanwhile, affected by the civil war, the American shipping industry declined, and the American government raised tariffs to increase national revenues, which hindered the development of Sino-US trade.

The reasons for the slow development of trade during this period include: (1) the recession of American shipping industry; (2) the establishment of restrictive trade tariff system in the U.S.; (3) the depression of American business in China; (4) the competition from Japanese tea and silk products; (5) the fall of silver price; (6) the aversion between China and the U.S. caused by China's labor problems and the Chinese Exclusion Law (Pan, 2013).

The third stage is the period of turbulent situation and fierce competition from 1895 to 1913. The Treaty of Shimonoseki signed after the Sino-Japanese War led to a greater degree of opening up in the Chinese market. In the absence of tariff protection, the open Chinese market brought a devastating blow to the domestic industry and commerce. The competition of Western powers for the priority of trade in China gave rise to the chaos in China's foreign trade, and China's industrial development, loans and trade were controlled and restricted by various European countries. The U.S. exports to China severely declined, but its imports from China increased steadily. During this period, cotton cloth, refined mineral oil, cigarettes and tobacco and steel machinery were the main exports from the U.S. to China, and the main imports from China to the U.S. were raw materials or semi-finished products supporting the American industrial production, including silk, tea, wool and peltry (Pan, 2013).

The fourth stage is the rapid expansion period from 1914 to 1922. The outbreak of the First World War cut off the material supply from Europe to China, and the U.S became the main trade partner of China. In order to supply war products, the American industry imported a large number of Chinese raw materials. In 1913, the American Tariff Act reduced or exempted the import taxes on lots of raw materials and commodities; moreover, the rise of silver price stimulated the U.S. to import Chinese goods. In 1913, the total amount of U.S. imports from China was $41.387 million, which increased to $176.471 million in 1923, with the growth rate increased from 100% to 427%. Except for 1921, China had been in a surplus status in Sino-US trade.

During this period, the main competitors of the U.S. in China were Britain and Japan, and other European countries were eliminated from the Chinese market due to the outbreak of war (Pan, 2013).

SINO-US TRADE FROM THE OUTBREAK OF THE SECOND WORLD WAR TO THE ESTABLISHMENT OF THE PEOPLE'S REPUBLIC OF CHINA

In 1931, Japan began its invasion and unbridled plunder in China, the trade in the occupied areas was rapidly colonized, and the development of Sino-US trade was restricted. In 1932, the volume of Sino-US trade was less than one-third of that in 1929, and until the victory of the Anti-Japanese War, the maximum volume of Sino-US trade

It can be seen from the above table that after the victory of the Anti-Japanese War, the volume of Sino-US trade increased rapidly and reached the historical maximum value of $558 million in 1946. After that, with the increasingly shrinking of the Kuomintang-controlled areas, the trade volume gradually declined. During this period, China's trade with the U.S. was in a deficit status and achieved import surplus every year.

Table 1. Volume of Sino-US Trade from 1945 to 1949

Year	Trade Volume	Hundred Million Dollars	
		Chinese Exports	Chinese Imports
1945	1.14	0.06	1.08
1946	5.58	0.93	4.65
1947	4.70	1.17	3.53
1948	3.93	1.20	2.73
1949	1.90	0.83	1.46

Source: Zhou, 1989.

Sino-US Trade from the Establishment of the People's Republic of China to the Establishment of Sino-US Diplomatic Relations

This is a suspension period of Sino-US trade. From the founding of the People's Republic of China in 1949 to 1970, the trade between China and the U.S. was in a state of suspension. The People's Republic of China was established in 1949, but the U.S. did not recognize it, and required some western countries to be on the side of it and not recognize the legal status of China. In 1950, the Korean War broke out, the military confrontation between China and the U.S. extended from the battlefield to the field of economy and trade. The American government took a series of political and economic measures to sanction China, and implemented cargo embargo on China, which completely suspended Sino-US trade for more than 20 years. When the People's Republic of China was just established in 1949, China and the US still maintained some trade contacts. In 1949 and 1950, the bilateral trade volume of the two countries was respectively $199 million and $238 million (Huang, 2005).

Table 2. The value of trade between China and the US from 1950 to 1970

Year	Total volume of trade	10 thousand dollars	
		The export amount of China	The import amount of China
1950	23812	9549	14263
1951	799	8	791
1952	5.3	0.3	5
1953	0.2	0.2	0
1954-1970	0	0	0

Source: Huang, 2005.

Then the trade relations between China and the US were suspended, according to the following chart, the value of trade between China and the US was just symbolic 7.99 million dollars in 1951, which decreased to 53 thousand dollars in 1952 and to 2 thousand dollars in 1953 even more. There was no direct commercial intercourse from 1954 to 1970.

The restoration period of the Sino-US trade, In the early 1970s, there were huge changes of global political and economical situation, the strength of the US declined relatively, economically, the US was undergoing the economic crisis and stagflation, faced the aggressive attacking of the Soviet Union in politics and military science, the US flinched, so that the diplomatic policy of the US, especially for the policy to China, changed obviously. Because the US needed to combine China to contend against the Soviet Union, so the hostile attitude to China was abandoned. The president Nixon issued a statement in 1971 that adopted practical measures to restore the trade between China and the US gradually and relieved the embargo of China. Though the value of trade between China and the US in that year was just 5 million dollars, it represented the trade relations between China and the US which had suspended 21 years started to restore and develop. Until Nixon visited China in 1972 and issued China-US Joint Communiqué, the trade between China and the US began to develop rapidly. According to the following chart, the value of trade between China and the US increased 76 times, which increased to 992 million dollars in 1978 from 13 million dollars in 1972.

The trade between China and the US in this term can be generally divided into 3 stages. The first stage is from 1972 to 1974, which is the rapidly restoration and developing stage after the rebuilding of their trade relations. Though the trade base between China and the US in this term is small, it grows fast. The growth rates in these three years are 160%, 1900% and 83% respectively, the growth of trade exceeded 35 times. The rapid growth of Sino-US trade in this term is benefited by the rapid improvement of the relations between China and the US. President Nixon took the improvement of the relations with China as the core of diplomatic policies; while China was isolated again after the Soviet broke with China and the diplomatic blunders in initial time of the Great Culture Revolution, in order to break that barrier and confront the threat of the Soviet Union, the improvement of Sino-US relations was also the important try of China. The second stage is from 1975 to 1977, in this stage, the development of the relations between China and the US was in trouble, because the Watergate scandal that led to the resignation of President Nixon and better relations between the US and the Soviet Union, the US attached less importance to the relations between China and the US; meanwhile, the wrong thought of left-leaning in China in this term broke the diplomatic policies and made the attitude of China to the US more cautious. With the stagnation of the development of the relations between China and the US, Sino-US trade was also affected, the value of trade constantly declined that the value of trade in 1977 was just equal to 62% of the value in 1974. China was in "import surplus" state. The third stage is the establishment of Sino-US diplomatic relations in 1978. In the late 1970s, with the global expansion of the Soviet Union, the relations between the US and the Soviet Union became worse, the US pointed at China again; moreover, the trade agreement signed by China and Japan and the EC also stimulated the US. After the Great Cultural Revolution in October, 1976, China had transferred the core of work to economic work; the normalization of the relations with the US was also the intrinsic requirement of developing Chinese economy.

Table 3. The value of trade between China and the US from 1972 to 1979

Year	Total volume of trade	100 million dollars		
		Chinese export	Chinese import	Balance of trade
1972	0.13	0.10	0.03	0.06
1973	2.60	0.40	2.21	-1.81
1974	4.76	1.03	3.73	-2.70
1975	4.71	1.29	3.42	-2.13
1976	3.17	1.56	1.61	-0.05
1977	2.94	1.80	1.15	0.65
1978	9.92	2.71	7.21	-4.50

Source: China Commerce Year Book 1984.

Hence, the relations between China and the US began to improve rapidly and the trades also develop rapidly, the value of trade in 1978 reached 992 million dollars, which is more than 3 times of 1977.

According to the table, the main feature of Sino-US trade in this term is that China was in trade deficit and it constantly enlarged as the time goes by. The main reasons are: the first one is that China adopted fixed system before the reform and opening-up, though it constantly adjusting the depreciation of US dollar, RMB was overrated seriously, and the huge domestic and foreign price difference suppressed the export of China. The second one is that the competitiveness of Chinese product is low, meanwhile, the long-term reclusive state led to that the US market and trade policies were known not very well by China, which blocked the export of China to the US. The third one is that in this term, China not only imported machinery equipment from the US to develop the industry, but also imported a good deal of agricultural products from the US to satisfied domestic consumption demand. So every year is the excess import year, except for 1977, the year when the relations between China and the US shrunk most.

The Changes of Trade Development of the Two Countries After the Establishment of Sino-US Diplomatic Relations

After the establishment of Sino-US diplomatic relations, the economies of the two countries spent 10 years' "honeymoon," the relations of economy and trade in this term reflected the developing situation of the political relations of the two countries, which are political tool. Frictions such as most-favored-nation clause, market access and intellectual property appeared entered into 1990s, while the fluctuation and friction of the two countries' political relations had not influenced the trade development of the two countries, no matter refer to the statistics of China or the US, the trade of the two countries from 1989 to 2000 has constantly growing, which the trade relations of the two countries gradually free from the constraint of the political relations of the two countries and entered into rapid developing stage. After China entered into WTO in 2001, the Sino-US trade relations entered into mature development stage, then the export of China to the world and the US appeared explosive growth for ten years. Benefited from the sharp increasing of export, a large number of surplus labors in rural China can go to coastal cities and work in export-oriented light industry enterprises, as many as 800 million people free from poverty because of that. Though the growth speed of export of China to the world and the US has slow down since 2012, supported by the US, the economic achievement acquired by China after entered into WTO cannot be underestimated (Liu, 2019).

The Sino-US trade speeds up recover and it entered into normal developing stage. China and the US formally established diplomatic relations on January 1st, 1979, soon after that, the state leaders of China Deng Xiaoping had visited the US on January 28th, 1979, they exchanged the views about international situation, property right and most-favored-nation clause and signed consul, trade, scientific and cultural exchange agreements. Sino-US trade developed rapidly after Deng Xiaoping visited the US, the enterprises of the two countries contacts frequently, a series of agreements that promote Sino-US trade development were also be signed, include the Agreement about Holding Trade Exhibition of the People's Republic of China and the United States of America and the Trade Relations Agreement of the People's Republic of China and the United States of America.(Chen,1979) The two countries signed the 3-year Sino-US Trade Agreement on July 7th, 1979, and decided the most-favored-nation tariff was provided mutually from February 1st, 1980 that made normalization for Sino-US trade. After Deng Xiaoping visited the US, the vice president of the US Walter f. Mondale visited China from August 25th, 1979 to September 1st, they signed cooperative agreements of enlarging cultural exchange and hydroelectric generation during that period, meanwhile, the US decided to set up consulate in Guangzhou and Shanghai to promote the trade cooperation and communication of China and the US.

Figure shows that during 10 years after the establishment of Sino-US diplomatic relations in 1979, both export from the US to China and import from China to the US have achieved significant increase and total bilateral trade amount also has gained large growth. After 1980, the amount achieved a huge leap. The amount of export from America to China increased to $3.823 billion in 1980 from $1.732 billion in 1979, while the amount of import from China to America raise up to $1.06 billion in 1980 from $0.6 billion in 1979. This increase could be partly attributed to America's change in its import regulation policy about China. According to related rules in Export Control Act, America divided its trade partners into several classes including Z, S, Y, W, Q, T and V. From left to right, each class embraced more relaxed regulation. China was in Y class with strict regulation on technology export before 1980. As China-US diplomatic relations became better, the US moved China to Q class. In 1983, concerning more about political matters, Export Control Act Amendment provided more relaxed rules on Chinese technology transfer. In 1986, China became the biggest provider of software technology to America.

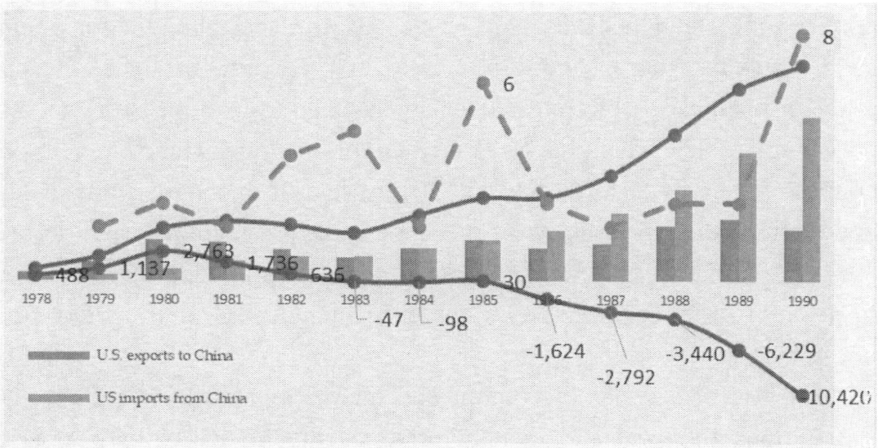

Source: Figure is drawn basing on data from the US Department of Commerce.

Figure 1. Sino-US Merchandise Trade 1978-1990. (Millions of dollars).

Figure shows that trade friction and conflict were unavoidable while glorious bilateral trade cooperation between China and the US was achieved. In the early days after the development of Sino-US diplomatic relations, United States trade with China was in surplus. But after 1983, trade surplus turned into deficit which grew up from only $47 million in 1983 to $6.23 billion in 1989 with growth of as much as 132 times. What is more, US foreign trade was in deficit as a whole. Under such a condition, America emerged domestic trade protectionism which led to disharmony between China-US trades. Statistics in figure presents that from 1980 to 1989, United States Department of Commerce and International Trade Commission have launched 17 anti-dumping investigations against China's goods in various sectors, such as chemical engineering, steel, textile and the like. Among them, the textile industry was deeply damaged.

Apart from the economic reason of trade deficit, political factors also played an important role in bilateral trade and commercial relations. Due to the short time after establishment of China-US diplomatic relations, considering the differences of ideology and state character between two countries, the United State put a cautious and prudent attitude to China, and communist state, which was mainly presented in a special regulation aiming at "Communist states," the 406th article in US Trade Act of 1974. This regulation stipulated that president has privilege to take measures to such communist states, which means that when International Trade Commission conducts a survey according to the 201 Article, if exported goods disturb and threaten the US products of the same kind, president has right to take temporary emergency actions to restrict import of this kind of goods from most non-market-economy countries even though ITC investigation does not finish.

Because of a series of complicated international political affairs like Revolutions of 1989 and disintegration of the Soviet Union, America imposed five sanction measures on China and political and economic cooperation between two states stopped, which did great harm to bilateral trade exchange. Figure also shows that in 1990, US export to China declined almost $1 billion.

The Development of Sino-US Trade in the William Jefferson Clinton Period (1993.1-2001.1)

As China deepened open policy, like the development of Shanghai Pudong New Area in 1990s, and enhanced its international strength, China-US relations of trade transferred to an inter-permeated and interdependent cooperative partnership from simple China's relying on import from the United States.

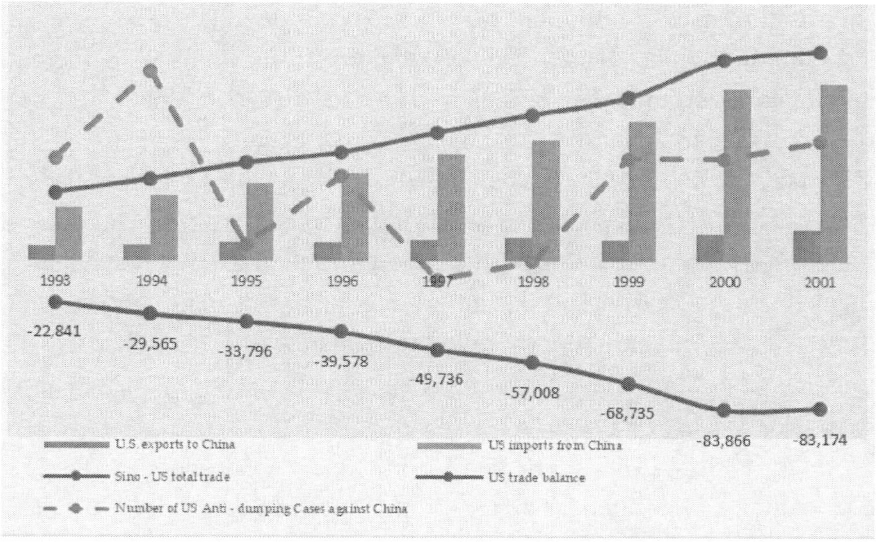

Source: Figure is drawn basing on data from the US Department of Commerce.

Figure 2. Sino-US Merchandise Trade 1993-2001. (Millions of dollars).

In order to adapt to the needs of foreign strategic transformation and industry upgrade, Clinton implemented Package Program of "New Economy" policy after his taking over power in 1993. Clinton changed the foreign economic principle from approving "free trade" to pursuing "fair trade", put forward "National Export Strategy" for the first time in history, and reinforced interference in export and protection to domestic companies, striving for more export chances for them. What's more, Clinton also enhanced the implementation of Comprehensive Trade Act of 1988 and the "Special 301 Article" in it, sanctioned countries having trade friction with the US, practiced trade policy of "multi-track system" and advocated combination of trade cooperation and communication which specifically presented in promoting operation of North American Free Trade Area, the development of Asia-Pacific Economic Cooperation and multilateral and regional trade cooperation such as GATT and Uruguay round of negotiation (Dong, 2013).

Figure shows that Sino-US trade situation is good in the Clinton period, featuring that exports to China, the imports from China, and the overall Sino-US trade volume all show a rapid growth trend. American exports to China increased from $8.7 billion in 1993 to $19.4 billion in 2001, an increase of 1.23 times in nine years. The US imports from China also increased significantly, from $31.5 billion in 1993 to $102.6 billion in 2001, an increase of up to 2.26 times, so we can see that with the deepening of Sino-US trade, the dependence of the United States on China's import has been more than China's dependence on US imports, and it's fully validates the increasingly permeable Sino-US economic and trade relations between them. In May 2000, based on the bright situation, China and the United States reached a consensus that the trade relations between the two sides upgrade from the "MFN" to "permanent trade partnership," which can be described as icing on the cake.

Figure shows the deficiencies in Sino-US economic and trade cooperation can be found. Obviously, the US trade deficit with China has increased year by year, and it has been a tendency continues to expand, which soars from $22.8 billion in 1993 to the $82.3 billion in 2001, increasing nearly two times. Under such a situation, the United States has carried out up to 50 anti-dumping investigation cases on China in 9 years, with an average of more than 5 and the highest number is 12 in a year. On the one hand, this is affected by the widening trade deficit; on the other hand, it is mainly due to the political sensitivity of both sides. Many factors such as President Bill Clinton, a leader of the Democratic Party, was often influenced by internal anti-China forces, the political interests and positions of the two sides are also different on the Taiwan issue, the United States, as a powerful political power, has repeatedly intervened in China's internal affairs, etc. have worsen the political relation between China and the United

States. However, with the deepening of economic globalization and the refinement of the international division of labor, the interference of political factors on economic cooperation tends to be weakened, and trade cooperation and exchanges tend to be rational and basically maintain a stable growth situation, which reflects that the US trade policy toward China was affected by the main interest of Sino-US trade cooperation and investment.

The Development of Sino-US Trade in the George Walker Bush Period (2001.1-2009.1)

In 2001, George Walker Bush was elected as the new president and reappointed in four years later. During the eight-year term, he was affected by various emergencies. Therefore, the Sino-US relation had ups and downs and went through about three stages. It's a low tide of Sino-US relation in January to September of 2001. In the early days of George Walker Bush's entry into the White House, the US government adopted a tough policy on China between "ring-fence" and "contact," he rose that China and the United States are "strategic rivals" rather than "strategic partners" in the Clinton period. In view of human rights issues, Hainan collision incident and the Taiwan issue, there are conflicts in different levels between China and the United States, resulting tension between the two sides. Figure shows that US exports to China, imports from China, the trade balance and the total value of Sino-US trade was essentially flat in the first three quarters of 2001, and there are few fluctuations among the three quarters.

It is a recovery period of the Sino-US relation from October 2001 to February 2005. The "911" incident compelled the United States to adjust its foreign strategy, and Bush quickly regarded safeguard national security and combat terror as an important task in his political career while he was aware of that China is an important alliance of the anti-terrorism forces. At the APEC meeting in October 2001, George Walker Bush formally proposed that the two sides need to establish a "constructive cooperative relationship" to strengthen cooperation and exchange in politics, economy, trade and military affairs. China became a member of the WTO in December 2001, and the United States announced China's permanent normal trade relation (PNRT) on December 17 in the same year, which can reflect the key role of the United States in promoting China to achieve a major breakthrough in the field of international trade. Figure shows that there was a significant change of the trade volume compared with the previous three quarters of 2001. The US exports to China rose from \$6.2 billion in the fourth quarter of 2001 to \$11.2 billion in the first quarter of 2005, nearly doubling and breaking through \$10 billion in the fourth quarter of 2003. US imports from China also showed a rapid growth trend, which gradually increased from \$26.5 billion in the fourth quarter of 2001 to \$60 billion in the first quarter of 2005, an increase of 1.3 times. Corresponding to the increasing US trade deficit, there are 8 to 9 anti-dumping cases annually for obvious trade imbalance against China. However, the total trade between the two sides is also growing.

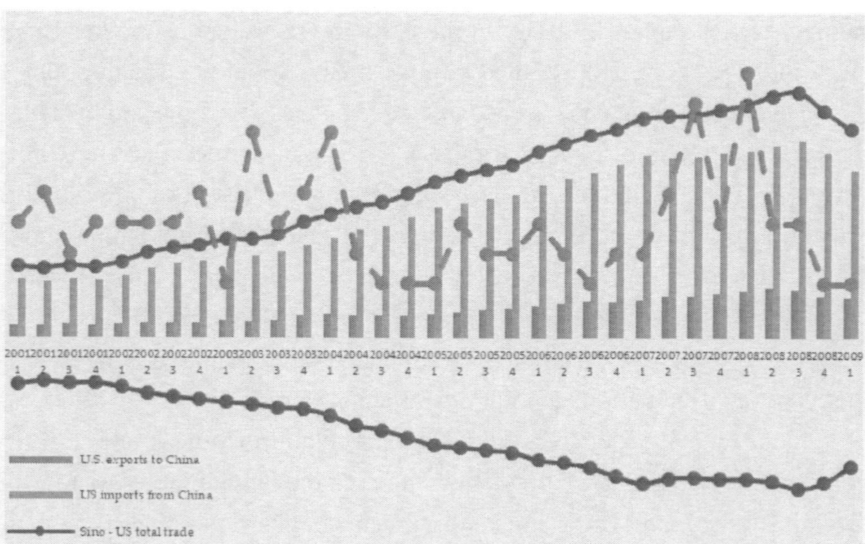

Source: Figure is drawn basing on data from the US Department of Commerce.

Figure 3. Sino-US Merchandise Trade 2001-2008. (Millions of dollars).

Sino-US relation developed steadily from March 2005 to December 2008. With the victory of the Iraq war, the United States shifted its attention to the rise of China, the announcement on Taiwan issue and the policy of "encourage India and restrain China" showed its defense awareness against China. There also appeared some disputes during their cooperation and development in economic and trade, including the United States exerts pressure on the appreciation of China's Yuan, protect intellectual property rights and punish infringement. Figure shows that the development trend of trade between China and the United States is basically the same as that of the recovery period. However, the anti-dumping case of US against China in 2005 and 2006 decreased rapidly but increased to 12 cases in 2007, while countervailing investigation cases developed from nothing, which may because the increasing trade deficit and pendulous policy towards China.

The Development of Sino-US Trade in the Obama Term (2009.1-2017.1)

In January 2009, Obama took the office, and it's a key period to prosper the economy after the outbreak of the financial crisis in 2008. The situation of internal and external difficulties make the United States has to re-examine and adjust its foreign trade policy. As early as the presidential election campaign, to fight for votes, Obama, as a leader of the Democratic Party, adheres to implement a more stringent trade protection policy and criticize many shortcomings of the free trade, but he positively positioned that the Sino-US relation is "non-friend and non-enemy" after he was elected, which can be seen in Figure.

According to the US-China quarterly trade volume data, the US exports to China, imports from China shows a growth trend besides few occasionally decline in the period, and the overall trade volume also grows rapidly which won't be repeated here. We can see a trend of increase and mutual-benefit in mutual-probe of Sino-US economic and trade relation.

However, due to the financial crisis in 2008, the unemployment of the United States increased rapidly, and coupled with its decades of trade deficit with China. To transfer the increasingly serious national conflicts and correspond to its re-industrial policy, Obama had created more trade frictions with China and made prominent policies. First of all, Obama used administrative and judicial means to strengthen the supervision and investigation on infringement of intellectual property rights against China, urging the establishment and improvement of the relevant protection mechanism. Second, the United States demanded for a more relaxed Chinese market, especially a more liberalized capital market to help their enterprises to settle in a broad area in China such as manufacturing, services and so on as soon as possible, and expand employment and reduce the Sino-US trade deficit. Moreover, call for China's financial system reform; promote the mercerization of exchange and interest rate to create a fair international market order. In addition, the United States launched a more frequent anti-dumping and anti-subsidy investigations against China, mainly concentrated in manufacturing where holds a huge employment, such as tires, steel, etc., and tried to set up new trade barriers to limit the export of Chinese products, for example, the carbon tariff on hand. According to Figure, we can see some relevant data.

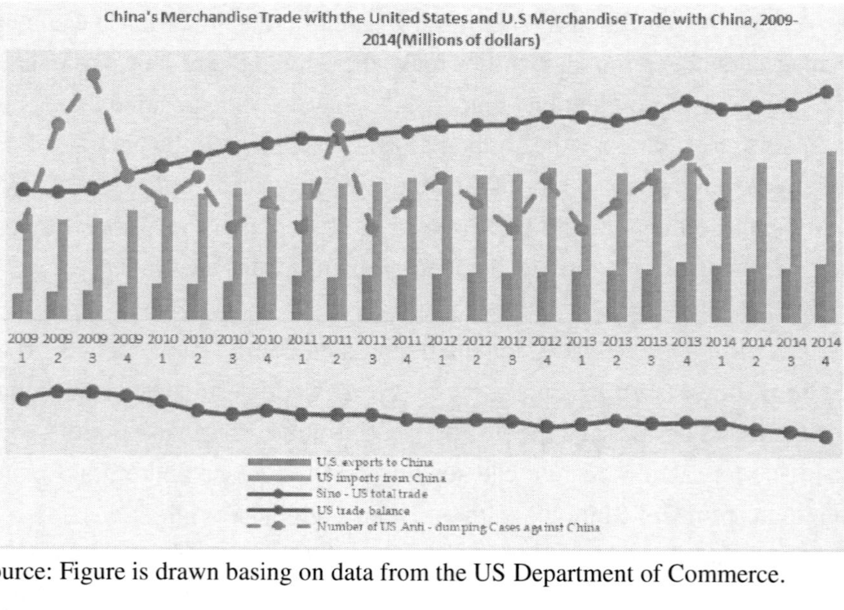

Source: Figure is drawn basing on data from the US Department of Commerce.

Figure 4. Sino-US Merchandise Trade 2009-2014. (Millions of dollars).

The increasingly deepened Sino-US relation makes China have chance to fully exert its comparative advantage. The US trade deficit against China continues to expand, and it has reached $83.4 billion in the fourth quarter of 2014. Frequent anti-dumping lawsuit against China follows. From the figure a basic law can be found. The US trade deficit will be reduced accordingly when the anti-dumping cases are more than the average, in another words, anti-dumping investigations have a restrain effect on trade.

Sino-US Trade Relations under President Trump

On March 31, 2017, Trump signed two executive orders focusing on the U.S. trade deficit (Shen, 2019).

Table 4. Exports and imports of goods and services from the U.S. to China, bilateral trade surplus or deficit

Year	The U.S. exports to China	Millions of dollars	
		The U.S. imports from China	The U.S. trade deficit
2015	164894	498189	333294
2016	170485	478574	308089
2017	187522	522889	335367

Source: Liu, 2019.

On March 1, 2018, President Trump announced to levy 25% ad valorem tariff on imported steel products and 10% ad valorem tariff on imported aluminum products. Although China is not the major direct exporter of steel and aluminum products to the U.S., it still filed an appeal against the tariff to the world trade organization. The first round of the U.S. tariff sanction against Chinese goods was implemented on July 6, 2018, with a tax rate of 25% and involving a variety of goods valuing 34 billion dollars, such as aero tires, water heaters, X-ray machine parts and various industrial parts. This tariff measure was soon retaliated by China's tariff on U.S. goods worth of $34 billion, and the tax rate was likewise 25%, these goods include electric cars, pork and soybeans. The second round of tariff sanction between the two countries was implemented on August 23, 2018, which was against imported products worth of $16 billion, and the tax rate was still 25% (Liu, 2019).

Meanwhile, China filed a new appeal against the new tariff measure taken by the U.S. to the world trade organization. The third round of the U.S. tariff sanction occurred on September 24, 2018, which was against $200 billion of goods from China, the initial tax rate was 10% and the tax rate increased to 25% since January 1, 2019. This round of tariff measure will increase the total value of Chinese goods affected by the new U.S. tariff to $250 billion, which is close to half of the annual total value of the U.S. imports from China. The retaliatory measure taken by China was to impose new tariff rate of 5% to 25% on U.S. goods worth of $60 billion, which increased the total value of U.S. goods affected by China's new tariff to $110 billion. Moreover, President Trump has threatened to raise tariff on another $267 billion Chinese goods if China retaliates against the new U.S. tariff, this would make the total value of Chinese goods affected by the new U.S. tariff to $517 billion (Liu, 2019).

According to the U.S. official statistics, the total value of the U.S. imports from China in 2017 was $505.6 billion (Liu, 2019). Therefore, if the new round of tariff sanction is actually implemented, all the U.S. imports from China will be affected by the new tariff. The impact of this Sino-US trade war on international trade and investment is not limited to China's economy and the U.S. economy, but concerns the global supply chain emerged and developed over the past decade. The trade war has brought great uncertainty to the consumption and investment decision-making of enterprises and residents all over the world, and may lead to permanent change of Sino-US relations.

CONCLUSION

This research analyzes the evolution process of Sino-US trade relations is sorted out and divided into four stages: Sino-US trade review from the Qing Dynasty to the Anti-Japanese War; Sino-US trade review from the Anti-Japanese War to the establishment of new China; Sino-US trade review from the establishment of new China to the establishment of Sino-US diplomatic relations; the development and change of Sino-US trade after the establishment of Sino-US diplomatic relations.

In the early stage of Sino-U.S. trade, although Sino-U.S. trade relations were inevitably affected by politics, Sino-U.S. trade was basically completed on the basis of reciprocity and mutual benefit, which made the direct trade between the U.S. and China, develop very fast in spite of the late start. Although the Sino-U.S. trade fluctuated in this stage, it was still on an up-trend on the whole. The trade volume of U.S. to China also increased by over six times from 1791 to 1841,although the increasing the opium export from the U.S. to China eventually changed China's overall foreign trade from surplus to deficit, China was still in a surplus status in this stage of Sino-U.S. trade for most years. In the following several stages, the status of Sino-U.S. trade changes with Sino-US relations.

Since Sino-U.S. trade normalized, the trade balance status has experienced two distinct stages. The first stage was from 1979 to 1992, and the trade was in deficit all the time. The second stage was after 1993, the trade had been in a surplus state, and the volume of favorable balance was increasing constantly. China's deficit lasted for 14 years from the establishment of Sino-US diplomatic relations in 1979 to 1992. This is mainly because China implemented the trade policy with import substitution tendency in this stage, and the restriction on import was essentially the inhibition on export; in addition, China had just opened to the outside world, it was not familiar with the international market, and the international competitiveness of Chinese enterprises was also weak, so the deficit had been small. However, the absolute volume of Sino-US trade was relatively small during this period, so the proportion of the unfavorable balance volume in the trade volume was large and reached the maximum of 59% in 1980. With the deepening of China's reform and opening up, especially after the establishment of the goal of building a socialist market economy in 1992, China's regulation on foreign trade management system has gradually relaxed, which stimulated the vitality of foreign trade.

At the same time, the international competitiveness of China's products is increasing day by day. Especially, the competitive edge of labor intensive products makes the value of China's exports to the U.S. increase rapidly. Since 1993, the status of trade balance between China and the U.S. has been reversed. China became an export surplus country, its trade with the U.S. was in surplus and this trend had been continuously strengthening. After 1993, the proportion of China's surplus with the U.S. in China's trade volume had been increasing, especially after China's accession to the WTO in 2001, the proportion exceeded 40%. From 2005 to 2007, the proportion reached up to 50%. Then after 2008, affected by the financial crisis, China's export suffered a heavy strike. Meanwhile, the constantly increasing labor cost caused by the appreciation of RMB and the increase in salary made China's export of labor-intensive products even worse. The growth rate of China's surplus with the U.S. began to fall. But in 2017, China's trade surplus with the U.S. reached $335.3 billion, which caused President Trump to sign two executive orders focusing on the U.S. trade deficit, and directly triggered the Sino-US trade war in 2018.

The imbalance of Sino-US trade is the primary obstacle against the development of Sino-U.S. trade relations, as well as the focus of the conflict of interest between the parties, and it is related to the divergences between China and the U.S. in exchange rate reform, market opening and other aspects. The trade imbalance problem is not only caused by the industrial transfer and economic development mode of the U.S., but also related to China's long-term development strategy of fueling economic growth by investment and export. The key to the normal development of Sino-US trade relations is too well deal with the problem of trade imbalance, and this requires joint and long-term efforts of both parties.

REFERENCES

Chen, S. B (1979). Talk about Sino-US Trade Agreement and Most-favored-nation Clause, *International trade issues*, Bei Jing, 41-43.

Dong, W. (2013). "U.S. China Trade: 1971-2012: Insights into the U.S-China relationship," *The Asia-Pacific Journal,* Val 11, Issue 24, No. 4, June 17, 2013, 35.

Huang, X. L. (2005). *The Trade Partners of Main Foreign Economies of China*, the University of International Business and Economics Press, Bei Jing, 19.

Liang, B. (1985). A Brief View of the Characteristics of Early Sino-US Trade, *Journal of Historical Science,* Shang Hai, 105.

Liu, G. (2010). Formation and Evolution of Early Sino-US Commercial Relations, *Journal of Chongqing University Of Science & Technology,* Chong Qing, 154.

Liu, Z. Y. (2019). *The China-U.S. Trade War and Future Economic Relations,* Chinese University of Hong Kong Press, Hong Kong, 3-4.

Liu, Z. Y. (2019). *The China-U.S. Trade War and Future Economic Relations,* Chinese University of Hong Kong Press, Hong Kong, 16.

Pan, X. L. (2013). *The History of American Trade with China* (1784-1923), Lixin Accounting Press, Shang Hai, 4-6, 10-11.

Pan, X. L. (2013). *The History of American Trade with China*. (1784-1923), Lixin Accounting Press, Shang Hai, 4-6, 53.

Shen, G. B. (2019. The Focus and New Trends of Trade Frictions between the US and China, *International Business Research*, Shang Hai, 7.

Zhou S. J. (1989). History and Status of Sino-US Trade, *Journal of University of International Business and Economics,* 29.

In: US-China Trade
Editor: John C. Amon
ISBN: 978-1-53619-956-7

Chapter 3

THE CHINA-US TRADE WAR AND ITS IMPACTS ON LATIN AMERICA

Adriana Peluffo*[*] *and Sebastian Villano
School of Economics, University of the Republic,
Montevideo, Uruguay

ABSTRACT

We present an overview of the trade war between China and the United States, highlighting the factors that have led to the current conflict. Subsequently, we discuss the key potential impacts on the two competitors, briefly analyzing the probable consequences not only on China and the United States but also on the world, particularly the Latin American countries. We illustrate how the trade flows of selected Latin American and Caribbean countries (LACs) complement each other and examine the possible scenarios for the relationship between China, the US, and the LACs in light of the new US Administration.

Keywords: trade war, China, US, LACs

---

[*] Corresponding Author's E-mail: apeluffo@iecon.ccee.edu.uy.

INTRODUCTION

China and the United States (US) are the two main stakeholders in the global economy today. In 2019, the US gross domestic product (GDP) was $18.3 trillion in constant 2010 US$, whereas China's GDP was $11.5 trillion. Since 1871, the US has maintained its position as the world's largest economy. It is regarded as the world's leading economic power because its GDP accounts for almost a quarter of the global economy, which is fostered by an advanced infrastructure, technological innovation, and abundant natural resources. Figure 1 illustrates the development of GDP for China and the US between 1980 and 2019.

China has experienced exponential growth over the last few decades, leaving the centrally planned economy and opening to the world. It evolved from a closed economy to a manufacturing and exporting hub at a global scale. China is often called the "world's factory" due to its big manufacturing and export base. However, the importance of services has gradually increased over the years, while the share of manufacturing in the GDP has decreased relatively. In 1980, China was the seventh-largest economy, with a GDP of $305.35 billion, whereas the US GDP at that time was $2.86 trillion in current dollars. After implementing its market reforms, it grew at an average annual rate of 10%. Although the rate of growth has slowed of late, it continues to remain high. Consequently, the economic gap between the Chinese and the US economy has narrowed rapidly. Figure 2 depicts the recent growth rates in the US and China.

It is difficult to predict how the China-US conflict will play out in the future. However, many analysts believe that the actions taken will have long-term consequences, even if the tariff escalation ends soon (Peluffo, 2020).

According to Evennet and Fritz (2019), there is an ongoing silent trade war, which reflects in the steady increase in trade barriers and restrictions on market access that have been percolating throughout the trading system over the past several years. The analysis of these researchers indicates that while the trade war in 2018–2019 significantly reduced market access for US exporters to China and Chinese exporters to the US, this practice of reducing market access is part of a much longer trend.

The most likely outcome of this unprecedented intense war between two of the world's largest economies is the grim prospects for the future of the multilateral trading system and the negative effect on most of the global economy.

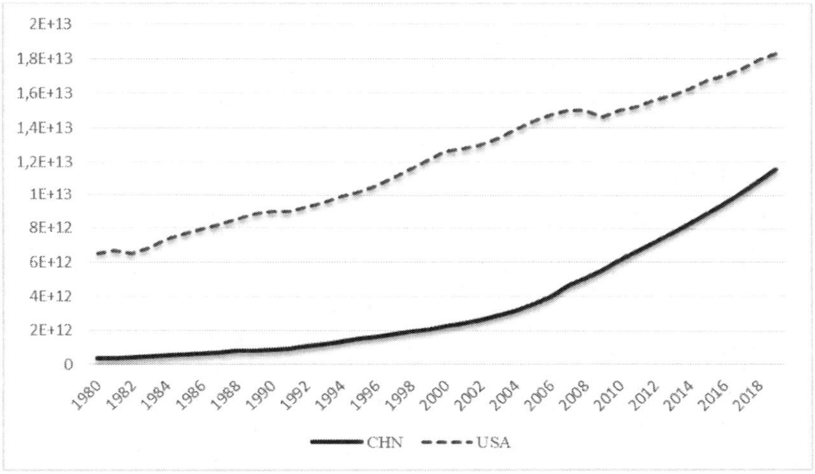

Source: World Bank, own elaboration

Figure 1. China and the US GDP in constant 2010 US$, 1980–2019.

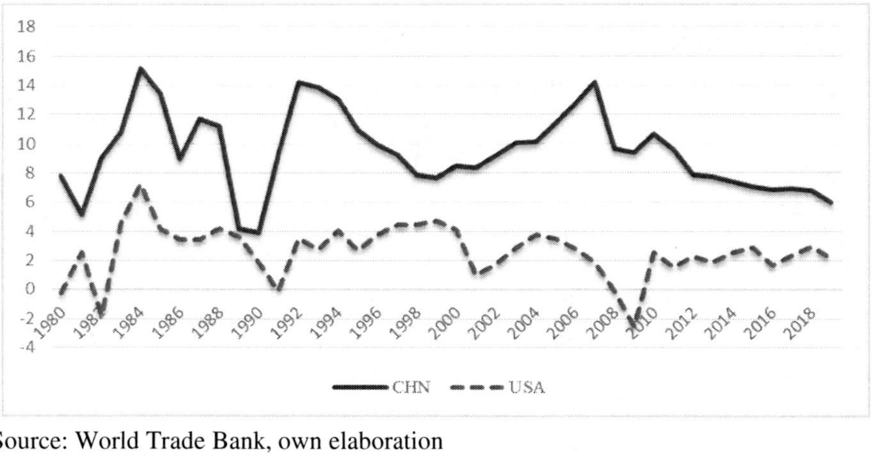

Source: World Trade Bank, own elaboration

Figure 2. The annual growth rate between China and the US, 1980–2019.

Notably, there are signs of changes since the new administration lead by Joe Biden assumed office, although there is a trade deal between the US and China, as we comment below.

Furthermore, the COVID-19 pandemic has shifted the focus away from an aggressive trade war to an American Jobs Plan to rebuild America's infrastructure, form unions, jump-start manufacturing, and increase competitiveness to maintain the US' position as the world's leading economy. Nevertheless, there is much to look forward to under this new administration.

Following this brief introduction, we will analyze the origins and evolution of the trade war. Subsequently, we will examine the causes of the trade war, comment briefly on the economic impact of the trade war, and finally, briefly discuss how this conflict and the relationship with China can affect Latin American countries.

THE BEGINNING AND EVOLUTION OF THE TRADE WAR

Over the last three decades, China-US relations have grown substantially with the total trade expanding from $2 billion in 1979 to $579 billion in 2016 (see Table 1, Figure 3). China is currently the second-largest merchandise trading partner, third-largest export market, and largest source of imports for the US. According to Li et al. (2018), the China-US bilateral trade and investment relations benefit both countries, as the US offers China a large export market, and the imports of lower-cost Chinese goods significantly benefit US consumers. Nevertheless, bilateral disputes between the two countries have increased during Trump's administration.

The United States has complained about the large trade surplus, ineffective intellectual property rights, and weak implementation of the World Trade Organization's (WTO) obligations. However, China has complained about the US export restrictions on high technology products, unfair treatment of China's market economy status, and unreasonable trade sanctions on China.

Table 1. Trade between the US and China: US exports to China and Chinese imports from the US in billion dollars

Year	Exports	Imports	Balance
2000	16,185	100,018	-83,833
2001	19,182	102,278	-83,096
2002	22,128	125,193	-103,065
2003	28,368	152,436	-124,068
2004	34,428	196,682	-162,254
2005	41,192	243,470	-202,278
2006	53,673	287,774	-234,101
2007	62,937	321,443	-258,506
2008	69,733	337,773	-268,040
2009	69,497	296,374	-226,877
2010	91,911	364,953	-273,042
2011	104,122	399,371	-295,250
2012	110,517	425,619	-315,102
2013	121,746	440,430	-318,684
2014	123,657	468,475	-344,818
2015	115,873	483,202	-367,328
2016	115,595	462,420	-346,825
2017	129,997	505,165	-375,168
2018	120,289	539,243	-418,954
2019	106,447	451,651	-345,204
2020	124,649	435,449	-310,801

Source: United States Census Bureau, own elaboration

The global economy has witnessed several disputes between China and the US. The trade disputes started in January 2018 when the US imposed safeguard tariffs on large residential washing machines, solar cells, and modules.[1] This led to a trade war between these two major economies leading to further retaliation and threats of further tariff increases, intensifying the tension between China and the US.

After Donald Trump assumed office in 2016, the White House took a tough stance on trade policies. In 2017, Trump initiated a "Section 232 investigation," citing national security on the import of steel and aluminum. As China is the largest producer of steel and aluminum, the investigation and the tariff imposed later were probably initiated to target China.

---

[1] Announcement available at https://ustr.gov/about-us/policiy-offices/press-office/press-releases/2018/january/president-trump-approves-relief-us.

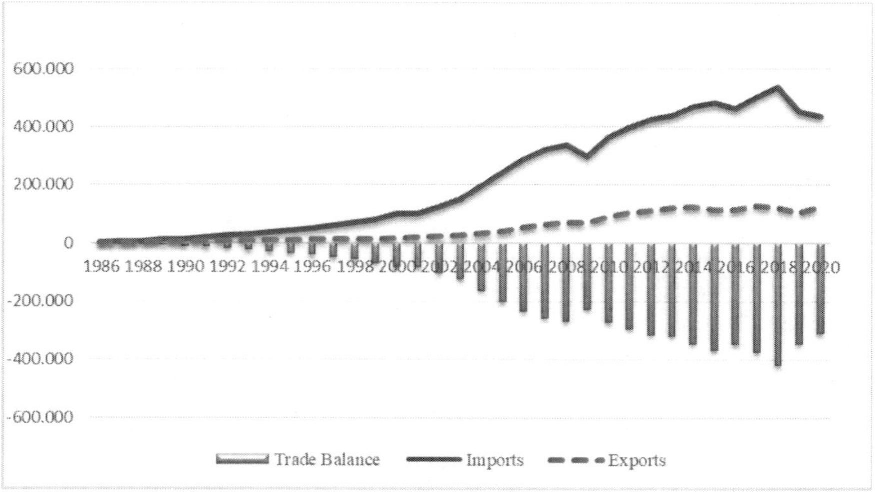

Source: United States Census Bureau, own elaboration

Figure 3. Trade between the US and China, US exports to China, and Chinese imports from the US in billion dollars.

Since the beginning of 2018, the US has repeatedly imposed anti-dumping duties or tariffs on Chinese imports. In March 2018, Donald Trump launched a "Section 301" investigation on China's intellectual property practices and threatened to impose further tariffs on Chinese imports. China retaliated the following day, threatening to impose additional tariffs on American imports. Throughout 2018, the US and China continued to dispute and retaliate by imposing trade tariffs.

At the 2018 G20 Summit in Buenos Aires, Xi Jinping, the General Secretary of the Communist Party of China, met with Donald Trump; both parties agreed to a 90-day suspension of new trade tariffs to allow discussions, thus initiating a sort of truce. However, no credible and substantial agreements have been established between these two countries.

Furthermore, some journalists and commentators suggest that the China-US trade war may eventually evolve into a new Cold War, threatening political and economic stability globally.

Although the trade war casts shadows on China's growth, given China's enormous economic expansion in the last few decades, it creates concerns about its impact on the United States.

The Causes for the Trade War between China and the US

Trade wars are not a recent phenomenon. Apart from China, the US States has also engaged in trade wars with Japan and the European Union (EU) over a wide range of goods such as textiles, vehicles, televisions, currencies, and steel. Generally, most trade disputes have been resolved peacefully with bilateral negotiations.

Usually, the economic impact of a trade war means a decline in export sales for the exporting country, which, in turn, puts pressure on the overall output and employment.

The influence on importers is two-fold; while some industries benefit from the protection of trade wars, other industries and households have to bear the costs due to an increase in prices. In most cases, the overall effect is usually negative.

Most trade wars in the past were resolved through negotiations, which suggested that the threats of higher tariffs were used to force the other countries to negotiate.

Thus, we should understand the underlying motivations of the trade war to evaluate its possible effects.

Usually, the true reasons for a trade war are not only economic (Chong and Li, 2019) but also political, such as the competition for economic supremacy between the countries. Among the economic reasons for the US are its dominance of the world, the trade deficits caused by trade with China, and the loss of jobs that were concentrated in some industries and locations in the US.

Pierce and Schott (2016) examine the impact of the US trade liberalization with China on American industries and regions that were exposed to policy changes at different levels. Their findings imply that trade tensions between the US and China have been exacerbated by the distributional consequences of US trade liberalization toward China, in which negative impacts such as job losses were concentrated in certain industries and counties."

The sharp drop in US manufacturing employment after 2000 differs markedly from the more gradual decline in manufacturing employment that occurred during the previous two decades. From 2000 to 2003, it fell by US$ 2.9 million (17%). Moreover, their research indicates that the implementation of US trade liberalization may have aggravated the consequences by concentrating the adjustment to the rise of China over a shorter period. Thus, the rapid decline in employment post-2000 may have exacerbated the distributional losses associated with tariff reductions on China by the US.

Furthermore, in this scenario, reallocating numerous workers is much more disruptive than when a few workers are affected. Reallocating numerous workers displaced by shocks in the trade policy may take longer, and the displaced workers' earning may fall abruptly, causing severe distributional losses.

The causes of the current China-US trade war are both economic and political, and one of the causes is the widening trade deficit between the two countries. As illustrated in Figure 3, the US had a significant trade deficit from 2001 to 2020.

The US trade deficit with China has been growing. By 2017, the trade deficit with China had become a major source of net imports for the US, accounting for approximately 46% of the total deficit. The trade imbalance has long been the root of US national debt crises and public discontent in the US, motivating the US government to wage a trade war against China.

As the China-US trade deficit has been a long-standing issue, not to mention the questionable effectiveness of a trade war in alleviating the US trade deficit, the China-US trade imbalance alone does not present a compelling case for the increase of trade conflicts between the US and China in 2018.

As Chang and Li (2019) suggest, net exports have been the main factor in explaining China's GDP growth. A close examination reveals that a significant share of exports comes from trade with the US. Since China joined the WTO in 2001, it has witnessed an increased growth in its exports to the US. Nevertheless, due to the rapid expansion of Chinese export markets, the contribution of US trade has decreased in recent years, although it remains considerably significant (net exports to the US alone represent more than 49% of the total trade surplus in 2016).

The trade war has also put pressure on economic agents, leading to a capital flow to China, which, in turn, leads to a drop in China's asset prices.

Another reason for the ongoing trade war may lie in the American political system.

In the US, during the midterm elections, voters elect members of Congress. These elections take place in the middle of the four-year presidential term and serve as a gauge of voters' sentiments toward the president. In the past, due to the "midterm election curse," the party out of power has almost always been able to gain voters from the midterm elections.

The midterm elections held on November 6, 2018, gave the incumbent president Donald Trump an incentive to adopt radical policies to appeal to his supporter base. The China-US trade war appears to be a timely and logical move on the part of his political party in the midterm elections, as one of Trump's main promises during his election campaign was to solve the problem of trade deficit.

Bown (2019) states that the failure to settle the dispute through the WTO may be at the root of the China-US dispute and deserves some blame. In this regard, the US has taken steps such as the following: imposing new tariffs not subject to international review by triggering the WTO's national security exception; retaliating against other WTO members without going through the formal dispute resolution process; and refusing to appeal to the standing WTO's Appellate Body (AB) if they disagree with a preliminary ruling. These US policy decisions from 2001–2018 have resulted in long-term economic and institutional consequences.

Nevertheless, China's subsidies and exports raised serious concerns, such as its worldwide domination on anti-competitive grounds due to its history of abusing international market power once acquired. Further, US policymakers were sensitive to the trade and technology-induced shock on domestic communities and labor markets (Autor et al., 2016).

Finally, besides the economic and political reasons outlined above, another reason behind the trade war is the battle for global economic dominance. As stated earlier, China has experienced rapid growth becoming a major economic power. China is now the world's second-largest producer of goods, and its GDP is greater than the US in terms of its purchasing power parity. The importance of the Chinese currency—the Renminbi or the Chinese yuan—has been increasing in importance in world trade and transactions, challenging the dominant position of the dollar. Moreover, strategic plans such as the Belt and Road Initiative and Asian Infrastructure Investment Bank to "Made in China 2025" may also have reinforced the image of China as a threat to US dominance. Thus, the China-US trade war has also been a contest for economic dominance between the two nations.

The new administration led by President Joe Biden promised a $2 trillion American Jobs Plan to rebuild America's infrastructure, create unions, and jump-start manufacturing. If this plan fails, China will overtake the US in the race for global supremacy. Biden has said that China is "eating their lunch," promising his plan would put them in a position to win the global competition with China in the next few years (Nilsen and Ward, n.d.).

Thus, Biden's domestic economic policy plan is also a part of his foreign policy to hamper China's growing global power. The way to challenge China is by making America more economically competitive by improving domestic infrastructure and investing in new and emerging technologies, namely in clean energy technology.

The US' competition with China is part of Biden's promise to bring middle-class jobs back to the US. The Biden administration officials have been explicit in projecting this plan as a major driver of job growth in the US across multiple sectors, including construction, manufacturing, and energy.

Nevertheless, Biden's approach is not without flaws. One is that China is a major investor in infrastructure, while the US has invested only a small fraction of China's total investment. The other factor is that, according to the Chinese government, only an authoritarian nation can move as fast if it needs to win the race, whereas Americans must obtain congressional approval.

While the Trump policy was considerably aggressive and aimed to reduce China's ability to compete, it engaged in a multibillion-dollar trade war, aimed at reducing China's prevalence in the supply chains of many industries, such as pressurizing Apple to move its production from factories in China to those in Vietnam. Further, it restricted the access of Chinese telecommunications companies such as Huawei and ZTE.

Nevertheless, we must not overlook the fact that usually, a nation is more united when it has a common adversary, and this can motivate both parties to do their best.

This reinforces the theory that the fundamental reason for the trade war is a fight for economic and technological dominance.

WHAT ARE THE ECONOMIC EFFECTS OF THE TRADE WAR?

Some studies have attempted to estimate the impact of the China-US trade war, and these studies have presented different economic scenarios estimating the impact of various tariff shocks. Among these studies, the International Monetary Fund (IMF) in 2018 found that a trade war between these countries will lead to a reduction of US GDP by 0.9% and China's GDP by 0.6%, leading to a 0.4% fall in long-term world GDP. Thus, not only China and the US but the global economy will also be affected by the trade war.

Guo et al. (2018) estimate different scenarios in which the US raises tariffs by 45% against China or the rest of the world, using the methodology implemented by Eaton and Kortum (2002). Gou et al. also consider situations with and without retaliation.

Li, He and Lin (2018) elaborate a model within the framework of the Nash bargaining and illustrate the possible impacts in different scenarios. These authors estimate a global general equilibrium (GE) and explore the impact of both tariff and non-tariff trade war effects. They analyze welfare, GDP, manufacturing employment, and trade using 2013 and 29 countries as the benchmarks. The simulation reveals that China will be significantly hurt by the China-US trade war, while the US can gain under unilateral sanction measures to China; however, it will lose if China retaliates. Under the mutual trade war, China's loss will be more than the loss to the US. The introduction of non-tariff trade barriers will intensify the negative effects of the trade war, and the negative effects on China will be comparatively larger than that on the US. Furthermore, the China-US trade war will hurt most countries worldwide, especially in terms of the GDP and manufacturing employment; however, it will benefit their welfare and trade.

Other works include those of Larzard (2017), Morrison (2017), Hughes and Meckling (2017), Schell and Chairs (2017), Dong and Whalley (2012), and Ossa (2015). All these studies reveal significant losses from the trade war for the US and China and the rest of the world as well.

Finally, the growing importance of global value chains (GVC) makes the costs of higher tariffs under a trade war greater in a trading system with GVC trade than in a world without GVC, and the distribution of costs across different stakeholders will also be different. In other words, GVC links mean that the burden of tariffs falls differently among consumers, workers, and firms involved throughout the value chain. According to some researchers, the trade war is much more important in reshaping global supply chains than COVID-19, the worst pandemic since the Spanish flu and the worst economic knock to the global economy since the Great Depression (Stangarone, 2020).

Additionally, some journalists and commentators suggest that the China-US trade war might eventually evolve into a new Cold War, which will affect the stability of the political and economic environment globally. The trade war casts shadows on China's growth because China has achieved huge economic growth in the last few decades. Thus, the future of trade and globalization looks gloomy. Nevertheless, it seems that President Biden's stance on the trade war is different from Trump's and is far less aggressive. However, Biden's approach to trade with China is unlikely to be significantly different from Trump's, in the sense that tariffs and other measures seem to continue.

Furthermore, the US and China signed the Phase One Trade Agreement in January 2020, which came into force in February and brought a pause to the trade war. Although China has failed to reach the purchase goal (it reached the agreed 82%), the US-China Phase One Trade Agreement came into effect on February 14, 2020, with China agreeing to increase its purchases of a range of US goods and services over a two-year period. Nevertheless, the agreement does not specify the consequences if China fails to meet the 2020 target. China has purchased large amounts of grain (corn and wheat) from the US. The large increase in Chinese grain demand has increased global grain prices to the highest level in more than six years. This increase is partially driven by the recovery of the country's pig herd after the outbreak of African Swine Fever in 2018, which led to the culling of almost half of the country's pigs.

The purchase commitments are only one element of the deal, while other components have also been implemented. Beijing has agreed to make structural reforms to its economic and trade regime in areas of intellectual property rights, technology transfer, agricultural market access, financial services, and currency and foreign exchange. Further, President Biden is trying to rebuild American leadership as an economic and technology leader. Nevertheless, all these reforms in the US and China do not seem to have favored American workers or investments. In 2020, China was the largest recipient of foreign investments surpassing the US for the first time. Moreover, it seems that the US-China agreement will continue during the Biden Administration (Piesse, 2021).

RELATIONS AND EFFECTS OF CHINA WITH THE LACS

Some studies have attempted to understand the growing relationship between China and the LACs. Wise and Chonn (2017) argue that from the Chinese perspective, China needs to internationalize its development strategy to compensate for its natural resource deficit, feed the world's largest population, and promote growth to become the largest economy in the world.

In 2001, China entered the WTO. The country has a high demand for copper, crude oil, iron ore, soybeans, and fishmeal. From 2003 to 2013, the unit price of these goods has increased nearly three times over a decade.

LAC countries that are abundant in these natural resources, such as Argentina, Brazil, Chile, and Peru, sell directly to China. However, countries like Mexico, which exports most of its commodities to the US and other markets, also benefited indirectly from the China-driven commodity price boom.

As discussed above, China's annual growth rate was 9–10% for nearly 30 years, and since 2013, it has slowed down to 6–7%, although the overall trade between China and LAC increased by 20 times between 2000 and 2016. In 2016, China accounted for 9% of LAC's exports and 16% of its imports.

China's rapid economic growth was accompanied by its rapid integration into the world market while LAC trailed behind.

While sometimes there is a negative opinion of China's rapid growth in the LACs, this also can be viewed as an opportunity for the economies of the LACs. This is not only because of a larger Chinese domestic market to export to but also because of the opportunities for growth in terms of new production possibilities, foreign direct investments, and financial flows (Lederman, Olarreaga and Perry, 2008).

The effect of China's growth has been heterogeneous across LAC countries, offering opportunities for LAC exporters and a source of financing. Nevertheless, increased imports from China have had an impact on manufacturing jobs and factor adjustment costs in LAC countries.

Table 2. Macroeconomic performance for LACs, 2003–2019 averages

Country	GDP growth (annual %)		GDP per capita growth (annual %)		Gross fixed capital formation (% of GDP)	
	2003-2013	2014-2019	2003-2013	2014-2019	2003-2013	2014-2019
Argentina	5.4	-0.6	4.3	-1.7	17.0	14.9
Brazil	3.8	-0.4	2.7	-1.2	18.9	16.4
Chile	4.7	2.0	3.6	0.7	22.4	22.5
Costa Rica	4.4	3.3	3.0	2.3	20.7	17.8
Mexico	2.2	2.2	0.8	1.0	21.6	21.8
Peru	6.2	3.0	5.3	1.5	21.0	22.0
Uruguay	5.1	1.6	5.0	1.3	18.3	18.4

Source: World Development Indicators, World Bank, own elaboration.

Furthermore, the specialization pattern of LAC has changed in favor of natural resource and scientific-knowledge-intensive industries. In Table 2, we present some performance indicators for selected Latin American countries.

The differential impact of China on LAC countries can be explained by differences in factor endowments and policies and institutions.

As Lederman et al. (2008) point out, there is evidence that at the aggregate level, the effect of China's growth on LAC has been positive, although some industries in some countries may have been negatively affected. The Chinese demand for commodities in addition to manufactured products, complementarities in trade flows, FDI, and innovation are the reasons why LAC countries take advantage of China's growth. Some industries will face stronger competition and will have to adjust, and this will depend on each country's factor endowment and competitive advantage.

In Figure 4, we present the overall trade, which reflects the exports and imports between China and seven LAC countries for the period 1994–2019. We divide this figure over the GDP of the LAC economies.

Furthermore, during this period, China's outflows of FDI in LAC were $113.6 billion (Dussel Peters and Velazquez, 2017).

We estimate the trade complementarity index (TCI), which indicates the extent to which the export profile of the reporter matches or complements the import profile of the partner. A high index may indicate that two countries would stand to gain from increased trade and may be particularly useful in evaluating prospective bilateral or regional trade agreements.

In other words, the TCI measures the extent to which two countries are "natural trading partners" in the sense that what a country exports overlaps with what the other country imports.

Among the seven South American countries, Mexico displays the greatest complementarity with China. This is due to the high commercial integration that the Mexican economy has with the US economy (See Table 3, Figure 5).

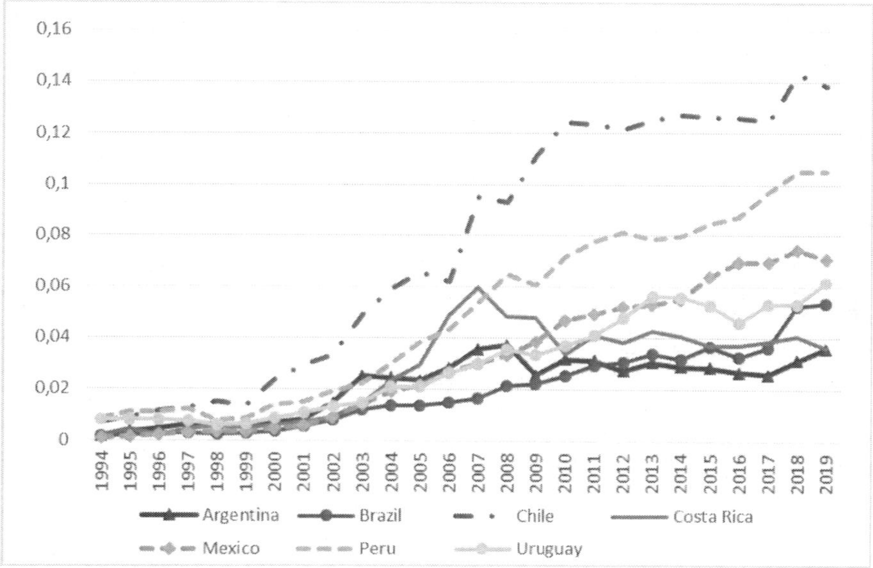

Source: World Bank, own elaboration.

Figure 4. Trade in relation to GDP (Exports+Imports/GDP) between China and the 7 LAC countries, 1994–2019.

Table 3. Trade complementarity index

Partner	2012	2013	2014	2015	2016	2017	2018	2019	Average
ARG	54.0	51.7	53.9	57.8	57.3	57.6	56.9	59.8	**56.1**
BRA	53.2	55.5	54.7	54.8	53.6	54.3	54.8	56.4	**54.6**
CHL	53.4	53.6	54.4	58.4	60.0	58.1	56.5	57.4	**56.5**
CRI	56.2	58.1	55.4	52.7	54.4	53.0	52.2	53.0	**54.4**
MEX	62.5	64.3	65.6	67.1	67.6	66.0	66.3	67.5	**65.9**
PER	53.1	54.0	56.3	58.4	58.8	55.7	54.8	57.4	**56.1**
URY	58.1	54.2	53.9	53.7	52.3	52.7	50.8	52.4	**53.5**
USA	*64.0*	*64.6*	*65.3*	*66.8*	*66.7*	*66.7*	*67.5*	*67.4*	***66.1***

ARG: Argentina, BRA: Brazil, CHL: Chile, CRI: Costa Rica, MEX: Mexico, PER: Peru; URY: Uruguay, USA: United States of America

Source: World Integrated Trade Solution (WITS), World Bank

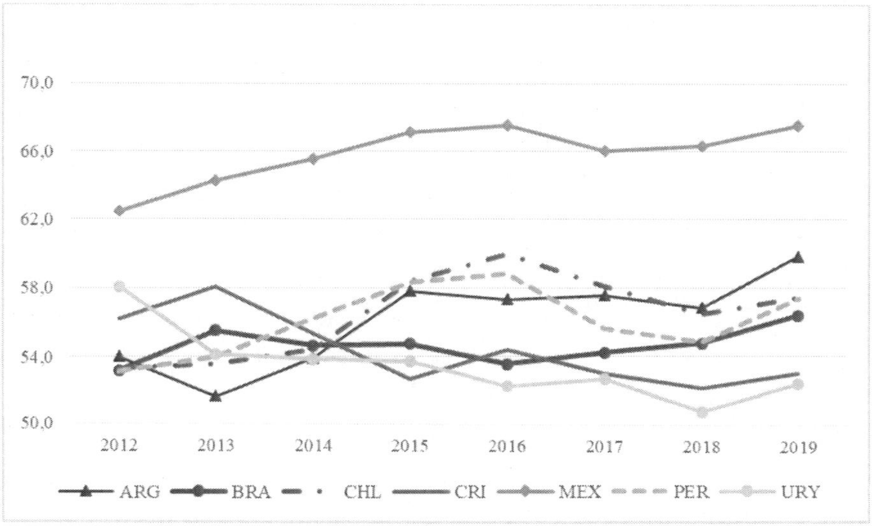

Source: World Integrated Trade Solution (WITS), World Bank, own elaboration.

Figure 5. Trade Complementarity Index.

The economies of China and the US have the highest degree of trade complementarity (on average for the last eight years, see Table 2), and therefore, a greater expected profit from the signing of a commercial agreement. The complementarity values are considerably similar to those of China with Mexico, which is consistent with the high degree of integration that exists between the US-Mexico-Canada (UMSCA) economies. More complex economies tend to have high values. On average, from 2012 to 2019, Argentina and Chile show higher values. Meanwhile, less diversified and smaller economies such as Uruguay and Costa Rica show lower but important values. However, Brazil's economy seems to be more of a rival than complementary to the Chinese economy.

According to Wise et al. (2018), regarding the political-economic dynamic that has been unfolding since the rise of China-LAC trade and investment ties in the 2000s, the two most common neo-dependency school diagnoses have been "unequal exchange" and the "resource curse." Unequal exchange refers to the dependence of LACs countries on primary exports—which are also more exposed to cyclical changes in prices—and the imports of manufactured goods with a steady rise in prices. However, the "resource curse" relates to a country's dependence on commodity exports at the expense of the industrial sector (Pastor and Wise, 2015).

In 1979, Chinese policymakers declared their reform and opening project and a "go out" strategy in 1999. As China has serious natural resource constraints, it has to incorporate natural resource-rich countries in Africa, South-East Asia, and Latin America in its internationalization strategy. China has several joint ventures with some LAC countries, and it is contributing to the development of some of them. China is currently a capital-abundant country pursuing an export-led development model. This is similar to how Japan, South Korea, and China led this strategy based on cheap labor, low domestic consumption, an undervalued currency, and huge economies of scale. Nevertheless, cheap labor and undervalued exchange rates are in the past.

Regarding Latin America, China's reforms could have an important spillover effect. Wise et al. (2017) report that the Chinese Premier Li Keqiang has made several trips recently to the region to solicit proposals for joint ventures between Chinese companies and local Latin American firms in high-tech and manufacturing projects (such as telecommunications, logistics, rail, and shipbuilding).

These visits have also raised the possibility of increasing Chinese industrial production in Latin America. Chinese investors are actively promoting the Twin Ocean Railway as a new dynamic trade and transport corridor, which would link Brazil, Peru, and possibly Bolivia. These capital inflows to Latin America are important and build capacity in the region to guarantee a flow of material imports to fortify the Chinese economy.

Latin America's growth in the first years of the millennium was based on the Washington Consensus (WC)—a market-based approach toward privatization, liberalization, and deregulation (Williamson, 2003). Although most countries followed the reforms dictated by the WC, these reforms did not lead to high growth rates for all LACs.

For some LACs countries (Argentina, Mexico, Chile, Peru, Costa Rica, Brazil), there were huge inflows of foreign exchange in the 2000s, allowing a decrease in poverty, increased credit, productive investment, and fiscal reform as we have presented above. Chile, Costa Rica, and Peru are three small open economies. Entering a Free Trade Agreement (FTA) with China opened new options for these countries while also defying these narrow neoliberal parameters.

Regarding Argentina and Brazil—countries with rich factor endowments and strong trade complementarity with China—they fell into a deep recession, and neither has recovered yet. Wise et al. (2017) argue that both countries suffered institutional erosion and reverted to reform during the Chinese boom.

Finally, Mexico accessed North American Free Trade Agreement (NAFTA) in 1994, dropping industrial policy and state intervention. This FDI-driven strategy has pushed Mexico into a low-growth trap and has left the country overexposed to China's competitive state-led strategy.

As depicted in Table 4, the smaller LAC countries (Chile, Costa Rica, and Peru) that were analyzed experienced higher growth rates and capital formation than their bigger and more industrialized neighbors (Argentina and Brazil) since the start of the millennium.

Notably, in the case of the three small economies, they undertook institutional reforms that included not only macroeconomic aspects and openness but also the modernization of fiscal currency and monetary reforms, indicators of institutional performance. All these three countries signed FTAs with the US and China. Conversely, institutions in Argentina and Brazil deteriorated in the context of corruption and recession. Moreover, these two countries played the protectionist game, imposing licenses on Chinese imports. In short, the post-boom period has pointed out the need for considerable reforms by most of the LAC countries. For most LAC countries, upgrading the technology, high-quality education, significant diversification of trade with China, betting on strong regional integration processes, and heavy investments in physical infrastructure are the structural keys to long-term dynamic growth (Ocampo, 2017).

Vianna (2016) analyzed the relationship between GDP growth in seven LAC countries (Argentina, Brazil, Chile, Colombia, Mexico, Peru, and Venezuela) and China's demand for their exports. The authors find that a sharp drop in exports to China for many of the countries in 2015 raises questions about the region's vulnerability to China's growth slowdown.

Santiso et al. (2004) argue that despite some exceptions, Latin America is a clear winner from Chinese global integration into the world economy. Using data for 34 economies of which 15 are Latin American countries for the period 1998–2003, the authors analyzed the trade structure of these countries and confirmed that there was no relevant trade competition between China and Latin America—they export raw materials, and China is a net importer of these goods.

Thus, there has been a rise in the South led mainly by China. This has left a significant impact on the world economy; however, there are significant differences among the countries of the South. Thus, the leading factor for the global South's emergence—and particularly the China-led commodity boom—brought tremendous economic and social gains to Latin America. Nevertheless, as that force fades, it is more pressing for Latin American countries to become better players in this new landscape.

The policy implications to help take advantage of China's growth and mitigate the adjustments costs are to produce higher quality and scientific-knowledge intensive products. To this end, further emphasis should be laid on education policies to help workers acquire the requisite skills. Additionally, policies to promote exports and FDI and help LAC firms integrate into global production chains will enhance the benefits. There is also a need for a social state that helps workers affected by unemployment during the transition.

The LAC countries will need to improve their human and physical capital as well as their technological capacity and business environment.

CONCLUSION

Today, it is difficult to predict how this conflict will evolve, except for the high likelihood that the actions taken by the two countries will have lasting effects. The Biden administration's trade policy with China is unlikely to be significantly different from the Trump administration's trade policy, despite the trade deal between the US and China. Furthermore, some studies indicate that permanent reductions in uncertainty over future trade policy enhance growth in trade and investment. Thus, increases in trade policy uncertainty (Brexit, unilateral increases in tariffs violating WTO rules) could also have long-term negative impacts on trade and investment. Crowley et al. (2018) find that tariff scare—increased uncertainty over global tariff rates on specific products—had a chilling effect on Chinese exporters that dissuaded them from expanding their export activity to new foreign markets. The reduction of trust between the US and China could lead to persistent economic losses even if a negotiated end to the trade war is achieved. Rebuilding trust takes time, and until confidence is restored, the uncertainty costs of this trade war will remain and affect LAC countries and the rest of the world.

References

Autor, D. H., Dorn, D. & Hanson, G. H. (2016). The china shock: Learning from labor-market adjustment to large changes in trade. *Annual Review of Economics*, *8*, 205–240.

Biden is using his economic plan to challenge China, Ella Nilsen an Alex War, Apr 26, 2021—Google Search. (n.d.). Retrieved May 22, 2021, from https://www.google.com/search?client=firefox-b-d&q=Biden+is+using+his+economic+plan+to+challenge+China%2C+Ella+Nilsen+an+Alex+War%2C+Apr+26%2C+2021.

Bown, C. P. (2019). *US Special Protection in Historical Perspective: 1974–2018.* Peterson Institute for International Economics Working Paper, Forthcoming.

Crowley, M. A. (2019, May 30). *Trade war: The clash of economic systems threatening global prosperity: A new eBook.* VoxEU.Org. https://voxeu.org/article/trade-war-clash-economic-systems-threatening-global-prosperity-new-ebook.

Dussel Peters, E. & Velásquez, S. (2017). Monitor of China's OFDI in Latin America and the Caribbean (2001-2016). *Red Académica de América Latina y El Caribe Sobre China (RED ALC-China).*

Eaton, J. & Kortum, S. (2002). Technology, geography, and trade. *Econometrica*, *70*(5), 1741–1779.

Guo, M., Lu, L., Sheng, L. & Yu, M. (2018). The Day After Tomorrow: Evaluating the Burden of Trump's Trade War. *Asian Economic Papers*, *17*(1), 101–120.

Lederman, D., Olarreaga, M. & Perry, G. E. (2008). Latin America's response to China and India: Overview of research findings and policy implications. *China's and India's Challenge to Latin America*, *1*.

Li, C., He, C. & Lin, C. (2018). Economic Impacts of the Possible China–US Trade War. *Emerging Markets Finance and Trade*, *54*(7), 1557–1577.

Ocampo, J. A. (2017). Latin America's mounting development challenges. *Why Latin American Nations Fail*, 121–140.

Ossa, R. (2015). Why trade matters after all. *Journal of International Economics*, *97*(2), 266–277.

Pastor, M. & Wise, C. (2015). Good-bye financial crash, hello financial eclecticism: Latin American responses to the 2008–09 global financial crisis. *Journal of International Money and Finance*, *52*, 200–217.

Peluffo, A. (2020). The China–United States Trade War: Will It Impact Latin American Countries? *Global Trade and Customs Journal*, *15*(11/12).

Pierce, J. R. & Schott, P. K. (2016). The surprisingly swift decline of US manufacturing employment. *American Economic Review*, *106*(7), 1632–1662.

Piesse, M. (2021). *The US-China trade relationship during the Biden Administration*.

Santiso, J., Blazquez-Lidoy, J. & Rodríguez, J. (2004). Angel or Devil? Chinese trade impact on Latin American emerging markets. *Trabajo Presentado En La Columbia University (Nueva York, Octubre de 2004), En La Georgetown University (Washington, Octubre de 2004), En Las Conferencias Internacionales Organizadas Por El Banco Mundial (Nueva York).* [*Paper Presented At Columbia University (New York, October 2004), At Georgetown University (Washington, October 2004),*

At International Conferences Organized By The World Bank (New York).]

Stangarone, T. (2020). Rather Than COVID-19, is the US-China Trade War the Real Threat to Global Supply Chains? *East Asian Policy*, *12*(03), 5–18.

Vianna, A. C. (2016). The impact of exports to China on Latin American growth. *Journal of Asian Economics*, *47*, 58–66.

Williamson, J. (2003). From Reform Agenda. *Finance and Development*, *40*(3), 10–13.

INDEX

C

D

E

F

G

H

I

L

M

N

O

P

R

S

T

U

W